LAMDA
FIRST FOLIO
SPEECHES FOR WOMEN

LAMDA
FIRST FOLIO
SPEECHES FOR WOMEN

Chosen by Patrick Tucker

PUBLISHED BY
OBERON BOOKS
FOR THE LONDON ACADEMY OF
MUSIC AND DRAMATIC ART

First published in 1997 for LAMDA Ltd.
by Oberon Books Ltd.
(incorporating Absolute Classics)
521 Caledonian Road, London N7 9RH
Tel: 020 7607 3637 / Fax: 020 7607 3629
e-mail: oberon.books@btinternet.com
www.oberonbooks.com

Reprinted with corrections in 2004.

A catalogue record for this book is available from the British Library.

ISBN 1 84002 418 6

Cover design: Society

Cover photograph: John Haynes

Printed in Great Britain by Antony Rowe Ltd, Chippenham.

Foreword

This Volume of seventy pieces is a companion to *First Folio Speeches for Men.*

Between them, they present many speeches from *The First Folio of Shakespeare*, with notes relating to their performance.

The pieces have been chosen to be suitable for auditions, and for use in the classroom.

Biographies

The Notes on the Speeches have been prepared by Patrick Tucker and Christine Ozanne, who together do the verse work for the Original Shakespeare Company's productions.

Original Shakespeare Company

The Original Shakespeare Company was founded in 1991, and presents plays with professional actors in the Elizabethan manner of no director and no rehearsals, with the actors only working from Cue Scripts. Working in this way, between 1991 and 2000 the OSC put on over 60 presentations, 29 of which were full length plays, in 5 different countries. The OSC presentations at Shakespeare's Globe in London were *As you Like It* (1997); *King John* (1998); and *Cymbeline* (1999).

Patrick Tucker

Since his first professional production in 1968, he has directed over 200 plays in all forms of theatre, from weekly repertory to the Royal Shakespeare Company. He has also directed more than 150 television dramas ranging from plays for the BBC to many episodes of Liverpool's own soap opera *Brookside*, as well as a feature film *In the Dark*.

He has served on the Artistic Directorate of Shakespeare's Globe since it was formed, and he lectures and teaches these ways of working on Shakespeare all over the world.

He has published a book all about the experiences and lessons learned from working with the Original Shakespeare Company, *Secrets of Acting Shakespeare – The Original Approach*, published by Routledge in 2002. They have also brought out the Second Edition of his earlier *Secrets of Screen Acting*.

He also co-edits *The Shakespeare's Globe Acting Edition* of the plays which presents, in separate volumes, the complete Folio text of the play in modern typeface, together with the full set of Cue Scripts for each part. Twenty-two individual plays are now available from:

M.H. Publications: 020 8455 4640.

Christine Ozanne

Together with her partner, Patrick Tucker, she has been at the forefront of all the Original Shakespeare Company's productions to date, appearing on stage as the Book-Holder (prompter) breaking with this tradition at the Jerash Festival, Jordan 1997, where she appeared as First Fairy and Starveling in *A Midsommer Nights Dreame*, and Lady Capulet in *Romeo and Juliet* in 1999. She has 'verse-nursed' all the performers in these presentations.

She was awarded an Honours Diploma from the Royal Academy of Dramatic Art in 1958 and has worked as an actress and singer in all areas of the profession, repertory and West End theatre, television plays and situation comedies, and numerous commercials.

After becoming involved with the OSC's techniques, she has given many lectures and workshops in the UK, USA, Canada and Australia, with both professional and amateur actors, teachers and students at drama schools including the London Academy of Music and Dramatic Art.

Christine is collaborating with Patrick on a new book to help actors called *The Actor's Survival Handbook*, also published by Routledge in New York.

Contents

12

Introduction

This book of speeches is different from any other, in that all the text used is from The First Folio of Shakespeare, and uses the original spelling, punctuation and line arrangements found there.

This is done because I believe that the Folio text includes, in its original form, particular acting clues that help all actors, directors, teachers and general readers, to understand more of what Shakespeare was getting at, and enables anyone to approach a speech without a long and tedious discussion of what the speech is about, what is going on around the speech, or what you the performer would do if you were in the supposed circumstances of the speech.

I shall show that the 1623 First Folio is an immediately accessible tool to the works of William Shakespeare – and is of contemporary relevance to modern actors, readers and scholars.

The claim that the original Folio punctuation and capitalization is a representation of what the actors said all those years ago is challenged by those who maintain that such matters were left to the whim of the individual type setter at the printers. They assert that the Folio details have no authority beyond the fact that the type setters were contemporaries of the actors whose spoken lines they were setting.

My observation is that *all* the Shakespeare pieces I have worked on over the years – whether they are in full length productions, in selected scenes, or in individual speeches – come over better, and are easier to act, when the original text and all its punctuation and capitals are strictly adhered to.

It is because of these results that they are highlighted in the Notes on the Speeches. It also must be mentioned that once some things are 'edited' to be more 'correct', then the flood gates are opened and literally thousands of changes are foisted upon Shakespeare's priceless Folio lines.

Elizabethan Acting

The Elizabethan actors who first performed the plays of Shakespeare worked a very heavy schedule, usually presenting six different full length plays every week – and introducing a new play into the repertoire at two weekly intervals. There was no director in the modern sense, and often the actor had no access to the complete script of the play, but was only given his Cue Script – that is, all the speeches that his character spoke, with just a few words at the start of each speech – his cue words.

My researches show that with this weight of work, there was no time for rehearsal in the sense that we understand the word today, and that the actors must have had a quick and reliable way of approaching a text that allowed them to perform as quickly as we know they did.

I believe that they worked from Shakespeare's text the way an orchestral musician works from a score – they too are not given the complete work, but are given their own notes, and they work from the clues in the music – not just the notes but the notations and added instructions in the scoring. William Shakespeare, an actor himself, would know better than anyone the problems of working to such a tight schedule, and I am sure that he wrote into each speech all the information that modern actors think they need to get from rehearsal – information on mood, attitude and character.

In the speeches that follow, I have written down a few Notes to point the actor in such directions as I feel Shakespeare has outlined – but they are not the sole clues to be got from the text, just the most obvious ones for each speech.

At the end, I have included an Acting Check List – an approach to acting First Folio text; a list of the main clues and how to interpret them.

Introduction to the First Folio

Read the Introduction to the First Folio – reprinted on page 20 – which talks of 'cur'd, and perfect of their limbes', and is signed by those who prepared it – two of Shakespeare's fellow actors and share holders John Heminge and Henrie Condell. They edited these works, and it is important to consider who they were, and what their point of view was, to discover the context of the works as printed in 1623.

All edited versions of Shakespeare – which make upwards of 2000 changes per play from the original – suffer from being treated as pieces of literature, and from being changed accordingly. The works of Shakespeare were written – and should be treated – as pieces of theatre. Reading them with that in mind reveals a whole host of ideas and points of view relevant to any modern performance or reading.

Although they say 'worthie to have bene wish'd, that the Author himselfe had liv'd to have set forth, and overseen his owne writings;' – it is probably fortunate that Shakespeare himself did *not* prepare his own works for publication, and maybe change his works to be more like 'literature', the way Ben Jonson did when he prepared his own Collected Works.

I often direct dramas for television as well as for theatre. Most theatre scripts are published, and are as accessible to the general reader as they are to me, but television scripts are only intended to be read by those who must interpret them – the actors, director, prop buyers, camera personnel etc. So the layout and terms used sometimes only make sense to the actual practitioners of preparing drama for the screen.

I believe the same is true of all the written work of William Shakespeare – the layout and terms used are specifically for his co-workers, and not necessarily immediately apparent to the general reader. Remember, the plays of Shakespeare were put on by a busy company, used to presenting six different plays a week. Under this sort of heavy schedule, Shakespeare himself would have worked into the scripts – spelled and punctuated the way they did then – those vital clues as to how to act and present each speech, and these elements would have been retained by the two fellow actors who prepared his works for publication as a commemorate to him.

That is why in this book of speeches I have used only the First Folio text, and start off by giving an approach to First Folio text, that includes those clues that modern performers of Shakespeare can use to let the original language augment the directing and interpretation. A fuller explanation of what each section means will be found in the General Notes to the Actor, following.

Patrick Tucker
London 1997

Heminge and Condell

The Introduction To The First Folio 1623

To the great Variety of Readers:

From the most able, to him that can but spell: There you are number'd. We had rather you were weighd. Especially, when the fate of all Bookes depends upon your capacities: and not of your heads alone, but of your purses. Well! It is now publique, and you wil stand for your priviledges wee know: to read, and censure. Do so, but buy it first. That doth best commend a Booke, the Stationer saies. Then, how odde soever your braines be, or your wisedomes, make your licence the same, and spare not. Judge your sixe-pen'orth, your shillings worth, your five shillings worth at a time, or higher, so you rise to the just rates, and welcome. But, what ever you do, Buy. Censure will not drive a Trade, or make the Jacke go. And though you be a Magistrate of wit, and sit on the Stage at *Black-Friers*, or the *Cock-pit*, to arraigne Playes dailie, know, these Playes have had their triall alreadie, and stood out all Appeales; and do now come forth quitted rather by a Decree of Court, then any purchas'd Letters of commendation.

It had bene a thing, we confesse, worthie to have bene wished, that the Author himselfe had liv'd to have set forth, and overseen his owne writings; But since it hath bin ordain'd otherwise, and he by death departed from that right, we pray you do not envie his Friends, the office of their care, and paine, to have collected and publish'd them; and so to have publish'd them, as where (before) you were abus'd with diverse stolne, and surreptitious copies, maimed, and deformed by the frauds and stealthes of injurious impostors, that expos'd them: even those, are now offer'd to your view cur'd, and perfect of their limbes; and all the rest, absolute in their numbers, as he conceived them. Who, as he was a happie imitator of Nature, was a most gentle expresser of it. His mind and hand went together: And what he thought, he uttered with that easinesse, that wee have scarse received from him a blot in his papers. But it is not our province, who onely gather his works, and give them you, to praise him. It is yours that reade him. And there we hope, to your divers capacities, you will finde enough, both to draw, and hold you: for his wit can no more lie hid, then it could be lost. Reade him, therefore; and againe, and againe: And if then you doe not like him, surely you are in some manifest danger, not to understand him. And so we leave you to other of his Friends, whom if you need, can bee your guides: if you neede them not, you can leade your selves, and others.

And such Readers we wish him.

John Heminge.
Henrie Condell.

General Notes to the Actor
on performing the Speeches

The numbers correspond to the Note Numbers at the end of each speech, under 'First Folio Verse Notes'.

NOTE 1: POETRY/PROSE

If every line begins with a capital letter it is poetry or verse; if the text runs on in a jumbled up fashion – it is prose. Poetry is 'heightened' language and your character is choosing to speak that way. By 'choosing' the end word of the line you automatically put the text into a metered pattern. (See also Notes 9 and 26.)

Prose is more relaxed speech and needs to be a contrast (theatrically) to poetry. Many characters speak both prose and poetry, which is a *big* clue for a gear change between the two.

Shakespeare often marked the major changes in a character by the moment they change from mostly speaking in one form, to speaking in the other.

NOTE 2: LONG THOUGHTS

Many of the speeches contain much longer thoughts than we expect. Modern editors have a tendency to break speeches up into bite sized chunks, but as a piece of theatre they play much better in their original long length. Keep the thought going until the full stop (but you can *breathe* without the thought stopping). The full stop (or question mark/exclamation point if the next word is capitalized) is the end of a thought – no matter how long or short that thought may be. If you highlight the last few words before a full stop, it will not only show you how long a thought you are embarking upon, but will give a hint as to what the whole thought is about. Find a way to keep the thought going through commas, colons and semi-colons, finally ending the thought only at the full stop. (See also Note 18.)

NOTE 3: COLONS AND SEMI-COLONS

The colon often stands for the word 'therefore' or 'because'. It is a way of joining up different parts of a long thought, so that the next part of the thought is related to the previous one. A semi-colon stands for the word 'and', and means that the next bit of the thought joins on to the previous bit. The important thing is *never* to treat them as full stops or periods.

Sometimes, a colon can indicate an unfinished thought, or where the thought gets broken. It is always an interesting acting note to come across one, and something should be done about it.

Technically speaking, a complete thought is a compound sentence whose different clauses are joined together by colons and semi-colons.

NOTE 4: SURPRISES AND UNEXPECTED PUNCTUATION

An audience can often see where an idea or a speech (or a character) is going. If they, the audience, get there before the performer does, then that is theatrical boredom. Shakespeare being the supreme theatrical writer, often takes the character in a completely unexpected direction during a speech – for instance, not building to the end, but building to three quarters of the way, and then undercutting. This makes the audience follow closely, for they cannot anticipate what will happen next.

The problem for the actor is that just as Shakespeare surprises an audience, he can sometimes surprise you the performer – be aware of surprising gear changes – and fulfil them.

NOTE 5: CAPITALS AND ITALICS

In verse, the first letter of each line is a Capital. Do not ignore the apparently random Capitalised words in the rest of the line. They are carefully chosen to give an actor's scoring for the whole speech. By giving them an extra 'choice' they are like stepping stones through the speech. (See also Note 26.) Words in Italics are either words of songs, foreign words or proper names.

NOTE 6: SPELLING AND PRONUNCIATION

The original spelling was phonetic. They also had many words with an extra 'e', such as heare, keepe, selfe, soule, againe, naile, walles, ribbes, which are to be pronounced the way they are today.

Where the same word is printed either with or without an extra 'e', then that is an indication of an extra choice or stress on that word. This means that the word 'mee' is *not* the same as 'me' – it is an additional piece of information to the actor as to how to perform it.

NOTE 7: ' ED' AND ' 'D'

Words ending with '-ed' or '-'d' are clearly printed according to the required meter, and to keep it they are pronounced either as ED (blessed sounding blessèd), or as 'D (bless'd sounding blest).

Example:

My Leige, I am advis_ed_ what I say,
Neither disturb_ed_ with the effect of Wine,
Nor headie-rash provoak_'d_ with raging ire,
Albeit my wrongs might make one wiser mad.

NOTE 8: ALTERNATIVE SPELLING

'than' was usually printed as 'then'. 'show' as 'shew'. 'I' can be either the first person singular or 'Aye' (as in 'yes') and Ile = I'll; do's = does and doe = do.

In the Folio they sometimes use abbreviations, so L. stands for Lord, S. for Saint – but M. could be either Mister, Master or Monsieur.

NOTE 9: MASCULINE AND FEMININE ENDINGS (AND ALEXANDRINES)

Masculine = 10 bits or 5 DI DUMs (the line ending DI DUM). You choose the end word. This is particularly important where the end word is one normally unstressed, or where the punctuation leads you to think about running one line into the next (enjambing). *Do not do this* – Shakespeare puts the end word there precisely to inform you and the audience of a particular meaning. If he had wanted the lines to run on to each other, he would have written them that way.

Feminine = 11 bits (line ending DI DUM DI), where the end word is weakened. If the last word is more than one syllable, the choice could go to the next to last syllable. If the last word is one syllable, the choice could go to the next to last word.

Shakespeare started his writing using masculine endings, but as his style developed, he started using more feminine endings, using the device to vary the lines and make them more organic. This does not affect the actor – if there is a masculine ending – choose the end word, if it is a feminine ending, then the acting note to you is that the final word is weakened, and you must make that a character choice.

If the line adds up to 12 bits, this is called an Alexandrine and the line is overloaded. The delivery can therefore have a squeezed or constipated delivery – you are trying to squeeze more thoughts into the line than the line can hold.

NOTE 10: ALLITERATION AND ASSONANCE

Alliteration is where the consonants are the same = 'be made more miserable'.

Assonance is where the vowel sounds are the same = 'any liquid thing you will'. These are additional ways for the author to bring certain words to your notice, of encouraging you to give them a little extra choice. You must create the character who *wants* to use those alliterations, and make those assonances.

NOTE 11: RHYMING COUPLETS

Some speeches are made up entirely of rhyming couplets; more often they will come at the end of a speech. Always acknowledge them by positively making them rhyme. The audience will be hearing the rhymes, and if you do not make them part of your acting choices, they will seem to be unmotivated, and therefore a lie.

A rhyming couplet at an exit is a wonderful thing – by really hitting it, it is like a trampoline that bounces you off the stage with panache.

NOTE 12: SINGLE 'O'

The single 'O' is not quite the same as 'oh'. 'O' is more like an emotion or exclamation, and can be expressed as a sound. The volume or pitch of the sound is entirely up to you. Most actors swallow their 'O's', as if they wish they were not there. Go for them!

NOTE 13: REPEATED WORDS

It is totally unnatural to 'just repeat' words without a good reason. So long as you say the second word (or words) differently to the first and your character justifies the reason for doing so, it will appear perfectly natural.

For example, with Lady Anne in *Richard III* – 'Set downe, set downe your honourable load' – say the second 'set downe' louder than the first, and the reason will be obvious – that is, her attendants did not hear her the first time!

NOTE 14: LISTS

If your speech contains a list (of any kind), always look carefully at the order of the list since Shakespeare deliberately puts things in an unusual sequence which can surprise you and your audience. Do not assume things build to a climax. Lists and whole speeches often peak before the end.

An 'illogical' list (such as Kate has in her final speech of *The Taming of the Shrew*: 'Lord/King/Governour'), might mean that the character is not as sincere as you thought.

NOTE 15: DOUBLE ENTENDRES

The Elizabethans were more honest about enjoying bawdy references than some of us are today, and a lot more of Shakespeare's words have bawdy double meanings than we now realise. A double entendre is just that, a *double* meaning – it should not be played as a *single* entendre.

It is not essential that the audience understand every Elizabethan sexual innuendo, but it is important that the knowledge that you are using a double entendre informs your attitude and mood – so if in doubt, twinkle a lot.

NOTE 16: BRACKETS

There are many reasons why certain words are put into brackets – and the main acting note is simple: just say them differently. This can include talking to the audience, talking aside to a different character; muttering the words etc. etc.

Brackets do not always imply that what is enclosed is an aside or a throw-away line; they can have the same effect as having the enclosed words printed in bold.

NOTE 17: HALF-LINES, AND ODD-LENGTH LINES

If you find a half-line in the middle of a straight run of regular verse, then the indication is that there is a pause required for 'business' or 'effect'. You may indeed find two half-lines which is a positive 'pause' clue. The implication is simple: since Shakespeare knows how to give you a pause (an unfulfilled half line), if he does not give you such a clue – do not pause, but get on with it.

An odd-length line (such as with only 8 bits instead of 10), means that there is a pause somewhere around – and the actor decides where in the line the pause should be.

An odd-length of more than 10 is either a feminine ending, an Alexandrine, just occasionally an Alexandrine with a feminine ending, or might even be an oasis of prose. (See also Notes 1 and 9.) Because it is not standard, it should not be acted as if it were. (For example, a line with only 9 bits could be seen as syncopated, with the missing beat showing where the pause is.)

Example (Viola:)

That me thought her eyes had lost her tongue,

could be spoken:

That   me thought her eyes had lost her tongue,

If the speech begins with a half-line, this does not indicate a pause to start with, but probably that this line finishes off a half-line that the previous speaker ended with – and so is in fact a clue to come quickly in on cue.

NOTE 18: MID-LINE ENDINGS

If the full stop comes at the end of a full line (but still in the middle of a speech) then a fractional pause is needed to think of your next new thought. If, however, the full stop comes in the middle of a line, you must finish the thought, but start the new thought immediately without pausing or breathing in order to keep the meter going. In other words – the new thought is already in your mind before finishing the old one. This technique produces a wonderful force to the character, and if you have several mid-line endings in one speech, it can have a really powerful impact and drive.

Sometimes (if it is followed by a Capital letter) an exclamation mark or question mark is also a mid-line ending.

A mid-line ending is like a charge of adrenalin, often meaning that you do not want the other character to interrupt you (as if they are about to draw breath to speak) – so get on with it.

NOTE 19: DIFFERENT RHYTHMS

Christopher Marlowe was the first major playwright to experiment with changing rhythms as an additional way of communicating with the performer. Look how the rhythm changes in the third line of Faustus' passion over Helen of Troy:

Was this the face that launch'd a thousand ships?
And burnt the topless towers of Ilium?
Sweet Helen, make me immortal with a kiss.

Shakespeare took this idea, and developed it into a powerful device of changing rhythms feeding changing thoughts and attitudes.

If the whole speech is not in iambic pentameters (5 lots of DI DUM), but in something different (such as 4 lots of DI DUM), then do it differently – sing it, dance it, what you will, but do not speak it as if it were the usual rhythm.

NOTE 20: SEPARATIONS

Where one word ends and the next word begins with the same consonant – always separate them: i.e. glorious Summer; Yorke claims; of Vertuous etc. This gives a little extra choice to the second word – and it is a choice that the author intended.

NOTE 21: COMPLEX/SIMPLE

Most verse lines in Shakespeare contain the verbal 'conceits' outlined in these notes, and should be observed and acted upon to gain full advantage when acting it out. The author, however, was perfectly capable of writing simple lines or phrases, which, when said 'simply' are greatly effective.

Examples:

Viola: What Country (friends) is this?

Lysander: How now, my love; why is your cheek so pale?

Lady Macbeth: Give me the daggers.

Cymbeline's Queene: Now Master Doctor, have you brought those drugges?

If you try to smear emotion on to a simple line it becomes untrue or sounds 'Shakespearean' in the wrong sense of the word! Someone expressing themselves with wit and double entendres, with metaphors and clever words, is someone struggling to express a complex feeling.

The gear change in a speech or character in switching between complex and simple language is always a wonderful acting clue.

NOTE 22: TITLES

If your character addresses someone in different ways, then the way they are said is not the same! For example, with Madam, Mistris, Lady, Cousin, Majesty, Your Grace, My Lord, Sir, My Liege etc. each requires a different attitude or gesture, whether formal or familiar, respectful or grovelling, etc.

Take particular notice of 'you' and 'thee'. They are not the same. You/your is more formal or public; thee/thou more intimate or personal. Sometimes you will change between the two within one speech. Try to physicalize the difference for the greatest theatrical effect (one way is to get closer for a 'thee', be more distant for a 'you').

NOTE 23: REPETITION OF A CLUE

Sometimes a particular clue (some alliteration; a mid-line ending; some bawdy reference) is repeated and done many times in one speech. This is in itself a clue – it is a large clue, and a large clue needs a larger theatricalization than a small one!

NOTE 24: ILLUSTRATING

Shakespeare was quite clear as to what an actor was required to do, as in Hamlet's advice to the Players: 'Sute the Action to the Word, the Word to the Action' – in other words, illustrate.

Many modern acting teachers tell their students not to illustrate – so you can experiment with either following them, or trying out Shakespeare's acting instructions, and see which gets you the best results.

NOTE 25: SOLILOQUY

A Soliloquy suffers from modern attitudes of 'talking to oneself', or even of 'talking to the invisible man'. In Shakespeare's day-lit theatre, this concept was beyond them, and a Soliloquy was when the character talked to the audience.

It is important to realise that there is no rule that the sense is the 'innermost thoughts' of the character – characters can lie or tell the truth to the audience in the same way that they do to each other. A complex Soliloquy, packed with double meanings and verbal conceits, is hardly a person sincerely telling the audience what they are really thinking.

When talking to the audience, do not talk over their heads, or to the back wall, but make proper eye to eye contact with many people in turn, and see how it will galvanise the whole audience.

NOTE 26: CHOOSING WORDS

When we say 'choose' certain words; as in 'choose the end word' or 'choose the capitalised words' or 'choose the second, because you said the first', it is up to the actor as to how they choose. In other words, don't think you have to stress or emphasise; you can 'choose' with de-emphasis, with pitch, pace, tone, volume etc.

The way of choosing is yours, the performer; the genius nudging you to choose is Shakespeare's.

The Speeches

ARRANGEMENT:

The speeches are arranged in the main categories of Comedies, Tragedies, Romances and Histories, and then alphabetically by play (the Histories are in chronological order), and in the order in which the speech occurs in that particular play.

There is an Index at the end both of the first line, and where appropriate of the most famous line in the speech.

All's Well, that Ends Well, I-1

HELLEN

O were that all, I thinke not on my father,
And these great teares grace his remembrance more
Then those I shed for him.   What was he like?
I have forgott him.   My imagination
Carries no favour in't but *Bertrams*.
I am undone, there is no living, none,
If *Bertram* be away.   'Twere all one,
That I should love a bright particuler starre,
And think to wed it, he is so above me
In his bright radience and colaterall light,
Must I be comforted, not in his sphere;
Th'ambition in my love thus plagues it selfe:
The hind that would be mated by the Lion
Must die for love.   'Twas prettie, though a plague
To see him everie houre to sit and draw
His arched browes, his hawking eie, his curles
In our hearts table: heart too capeable
Of everie line and tricke of his sweet favour.
But now he's gone, and my idolatrous fancie
Must sanctifie his Reliques.   Who comes heere?

ENTER PAROLLES.

One that goes with him: I love him for his sake,
And yet I know him a notorious Liar,
Thinke him a great way foole, solie a coward,
Yet these fixt evils sit so fit in him,
That they take place, when Vertues steely bones
Lookes bleake i'th cold wind: withall, full ofte we see
Cold wisedome waighting on superfluous folie.

FIRST FOLIO VERSE NOTES

The speech starts with an 'O': **See Note 12**.

The 2nd line's separation 'great teares' focus the start of the speech: **See Note 20**, and there is another good separation in 'his sphere', and 'his sweet'.

Using the end words of each line works well for this speech: **See Note 9**.

There are 4 mid-line endings to give the drive to the whole: **See Note 18**.

The complexity of the speech switches suddenly to a great simplicity in the last line before Parrolles enters: **See Note 21**.

The remaining 8 lines are all one thought leading to the last line's heavy condemnation: **See Note 2.**

All's Well, that Ends Well, I-3

HELLEN

Then I confesse
Here on my knee, before high heaven and you,
That before you, and next unto high heaven, I love your
                                        Sonne:
My friends were poore but honest, so's my love:
Be not offended, for it hurts not him
That he is lov'd of me; I follow him not
By any token of presumptuous suite,
Nor would I have him, till I doe deserve him,
Yet never know how that desert should be:
I know I love in vaine, strive against hope:
Yet in this captious, and intemible Sive,
I still poure in the waters of my love
And lacke not to loose still; thus *Indian* like
Religious in mine error, I adore
The Sunne that lookes upon his worshipper,
But knowes of him no more.   My deerest Madam,
Let not your hate incounter with my love,
For loving where you doe; but if your selfe,
Whose aged honor cites a vertuous youth,
Did ever, in so true a flame of liking,
Wish chastly, and love dearely, that your *Dian*
Was both her selfe and love, O then give pittie
To her whose state is such, that cannot choose
But lend and give where she is sure to loose;
That seekes not to finde that, her search implies,
But riddle like, lives sweetely where she dies.

FIRST FOLIO VERSE NOTES:

The first full stop is a good 16 lines into the speech: **See Note 2**, and then it is in the middle of a line: **See Note 18**.

The colons in the speech all point towards the argument: **See Note 3**.

The end words of each line are particularly important: **See Note 9**.

The third line: 'That before you ...' is particularly long: **See Note 17**.

There is a pun throughout on the words 'Sonne' and 'Sunne', and the '-ed' endings such as in 'aged' need to be spoken: **See Note 7**.

Towards the end she has a wonderful 'O': **See Note 12**.

The speech ends with 2 sets of rhyming couplets: **See Note 11**.

All's Well, that Ends Well, III-2

HELLEN

Till I have no wife I have nothing in France.
Nothing in France untill he has no wife:
Thou shalt have none *Rossillion*, none in France,
Then hast thou all againe: poore Lord, is't I
That chase thee from thy Countrie, and expose
Those tender limbes of thine, to the event
Of the none-sparing warre?   And is it I,
That drive thee from the sportive Court, where thou
Was't shot at with faire eyes, to be the marke
Of smoakie Muskets?   O you leaden messengers,
That ride upon the violent speede of fire,
Fly with false ayme, move the still-peering aire
That sings with piercing, do not touch my Lord:
Who ever shoots at him, I set him there.
Who ever charges on his forward brest
I am the Caitiffe that do hold him too't,
And though I kill him not, I am the cause
His death was so effected: Better 'twere
I met the ravine Lyon when he roar'd
With sharpe constraint of hunger: better 'twere,
That all the miseries which nature owes
Were mine at once.   No come thou home *Rossillion*,
Whence honor but of danger winnes a scarre,
As oft it looses all.   I will be gone:
My being heere it is, that holds thee hence,
Shall I stay heere to doo't?   No, no, although
The ayre of Paradise did fan the house,
And Angels offic'd all: I will be gone,
That pittifull rumour may report my flight
To consolate thine eare.   Come night, end day,
For with the darke (poore theefe) Ile steale away.

FIRST FOLIO VERSE NOTES:

The italics at the start show she is reading from a letter: **See Note 5**.

It is a soliloquy: **See Note 25**.

There is also a nice 'O' in the middle: **See Note 12**.

The ends words of the speech are particularly important: **See Note 9**, and the tenth line is an Alexandrine.

The assonances of 'I/drive/eyes' point up the passion in the speech: **See Note 10**.

There are 6 mid-line endings in the piece: **See Notes 18 & 23**.

As you Like it, III-5

ROSALIND

And why I pray you? who might be your mother
That you insult, exult, and all at once
Over the wretched? what though you hav no beauty
As by my faith, I see no more in you
Then without Candle may goe darke to bed:
Must you be therefore prowd and pittilesse?
Why what meanes this? why do you looke on me?
I see no more in you then in the ordinary
Of Natures sale-worke? 'ods my little life,
I thinke she meanes to tangle my eies too:
No faith proud Mistresse, hope not after it,
'Tis not your inkie browes, your blacke silke haire,
Your bugle eye-balls, nor your cheeke of creame
That can entame my spirits to your worship:
You foolish Shepheard, wherefore do you follow her
Like foggy South, puffing with winde and raine,
You are a thousand times a properer man
Then she a woman.   'Tis such fooles as you
That makes the world full of ill-favourd children:
'Tis not her glasse, but you that flatters her,
And out of you she sees her selfe more proper
Then any of her lineaments can show her:
But Mistris, know your selfe, downe on your knees
And thanke heaven, fasting, for a good mans love;
For I must tell you friendly in your eare,
Sell when you can, you are not for all markets:
Cry the man mercy, love him, take his offer,
Foule is most foule, being foule to be a scoffer.
So take her to thee Shepheard, fareyouwell.

FIRST FOLIO VERSE NOTES:

The assonance of 'why/I' in the first line shows the drive of the speech: **See Note 10**.

In particular, the end words in the speech need to be chosen: **See Note 9**.

The speech is 2 long thoughts, with a mid-line ending: **See Notes 2 & 18**.

One of the listeners is referred to as 'you', and in the last line the other as 'thee': **See Note 22**.

There are a lot of question marks in the speech; make sure they are acted *as* questions.

''ods' = God save

As you Like it, III-5

PHEBE

Thinke not I love him, though I ask for him,
'Tis but a peevish boy, yet he talkes well,
But what care I for words? yet words do well
When he that speakes them pleases those that heare:
It is a pretty youth, not very prettie,
But sure hee's proud, and yet his pride becomes him;
Hee'll make a proper man: the best thing in him
Is his complexion: and faster then his tongue
Did make offence, his eye did heale it up:
He is not very tall, yet for his yeeres hee's tall:
His leg is but so so, and yet 'tis well:
There was a pretty rednesse in his lip,
A little riper, and more lustie red
Then that mixt in his cheeke: 'twas just the difference
Betwixt the constant red, and mingled Damaske.
There be some women *Silvius*, had they markt him
In parcells as I did, would have gone neere
To fall in love with him: but for my part
I love him not, nor hate him not: and yet
Have more cause to hate him then to love him,
For what had he to doe to chide at me?
He said mine eyes were black, and my haire blacke,
And now I am remembred, scorn'd at me:
I marvell why I answer'd not againe,
But that's all one: omittance is no quittance:
Ile write to him a very tanting Letter,
And thou shalt beare it, wilt thou *Silvius*?

FIRST FOLIO VERSE NOTES:

The speech keeps going for 15 lines until 'Damaske': **See Note 2**, and the colons and semi-colons sort out the argument: **See Note 3**.

The speech is full of assonances and alliterations, such as 'he/speakes/pleases': **See Note 10**.

The spelling as in 'hee's proud'; and 'hee'll make a proper man' shows the emphasis: **See Note 6**.

The word 'proud' can also mean 'bulging', which gives an interesting slant onto what she is saying: **See Note 15**.

'Tanting' = taunting.

As you Like it, V-4

ROSALIND

It is not the fashion to see the Ladie the Epilogue: but it is no more unhandsome, then to see the
Lord the Prologue. If it be true, that good wine needs
no bush, 'tis true, that a good play needes no Epilogue.
Yet to good wine they do use good bushes: and good
playes prove the better by the helpe of good Epilogues:
What a case am I in then, that am neither a good Epilogue, nor cannot insinuate with you in the behalfe of a
good play? I am not furnish'd like a Begger, therefore
to begge will not become mee. My way is to conjure
you, and Ile begin with the Women. I charge you (O
women) for the love you beare to men, to like as much
of this Play, as please you: And I charge you (O men)
for the love you beare to women (as I perceive by your
simpring, none of you hates them) that betweene you,
and the women, the play may please. If I were a Woman, I would kisse as many of you as had beards that
pleas'd me, complexions that lik'd me, and breaths that
I defi'de not: And I am sure, as many as have good
beards, or good faces, or sweet breaths, will for my kind
offer, when I make curt'sie, bid me farewell.

FIRST FOLIO VERSE NOTES:

The speech is all in prose: **See Note 1**, and is a soliloquy: **See Note 25**.

The capitals are a good guide through the speech: **See Note 5**.

The single 'O's' should be used: **See Note 12**, and there are 3 sets of brackets that need to be acknowledged: **See Note 16**.

The long spelling of 'mee' is there to be used: **See Note 6**.

In those days they used to hang a bush outside a building, to indicate it was a pub or inn.

The Comedie of Errors, II-2

ADRIANA

I, I, *Antipholus*, looke strange and frowne,
Some other Mistresse hath thy sweet aspects:
I am not *Adriana*, nor thy wife.
The time was once, when thou un-urg'd wouldst vow,
That never words were musicke to thine eare,
That never object pleasing in thine eye,
That never touch well welcome to thy hand,
That never meat sweet-savour'd in thy taste,
Unlesse I spake, or look'd, or touch'd, or carv'd to thee.
How comes it now, my Husband, oh how comes it,
That thou art then estranged from thy selfe?
Thy selfe I call it, being strange to me:
That undividable Incorporate
Am better then thy deere selfes better part.
Ah doe not teare away thy selfe from me;
For know my love: as easie maist thou fall
A drop of water in the breaking gulfe,
And take unmingled thence that drop againe
Without addition or diminishing,
As take from me thy selfe, and not me too.
How deerely would it touch thee to the quicke,
Shouldst thou but heare I were licencious?
And that this body consecrate to thee,
By Ruffian Lust should be contaminate?
Wouldst thou not spit at me, and spurne at me,
And hurle the name of husband in my face,
And teare the stain'd skin of my Harlot brow,
And from my false hand cut the wedding ring,
And breake it with a deepe-divorcing vow?
I know thou canst, and therefore see thou doe it.
I am possest with an adulterate blot,
My bloud is mingled with the crime of lust:

For if we two be one, and thou play false,
I doe digest the poison of thy flesh,
Being strumpeted by thy contagion.
Keepe then faire league and truce with thy true bed,
I live distain'd, thou undishonoured.

FIRST FOLIO VERSE NOTES:

The speech starts with a choice – is it 'I' or 'Aye'?: **See Notes 6 & 13**, and the word 'I' is repeated a lot more in this speech.

There are 4 repetitions of the phrase 'That never', and 4 lines in a row start with 'And': **See Note 13**.

The '-ed' endings need to be used, such as 'estranged', 'unmingled', and 'undishonoured': **See Note 7**.

The colons in the speech show which bit of the argument belongs to which: **See Note 3**.

The alliterations of 'hurle/husband/Harlot' show the build in emotion: **See Note 10**.

The speech ends with a rhyming couplet: **See Note 11**.

Editors change 'of my Harlot brow' to 'off my Harlot brow'.

The Comedie of Errors, III-2

LUCIANA

And may it be that you have quite forgot
A husbands office? shall *Antipholus*
Even in the spring of Love, thy Love-springs rot?
Shall love in buildings grow so ruinate?
If you did wed my sister for her wealth,
Then for her wealths-sake use her with more kindnesse:
Or if you like else-where doe it by stealth,
Muffle your false love with some shew of blindnesse:
Let not my sister read it in your eye:
Be not thy tongue thy owne shames Orator:
Looke sweet, speake faire, become disloyaltie:
Apparell vice like vertues harbenger:
Beare a faire presence, though your heart be tainted,
Teach sinne the carriage of a holy Saint,
Be secret false: what need she be acquainted?
What simple thiefe brags of his owne attaine?
'Tis double wrong to truant with your bed,
And let her read it in thy lookes at boord:
Shame hath a bastard fame, well managed,
Ill deeds is doubled with an evill word:
Alas poore women, make us not beleeve
(Being compact of credit) that you love us,
Though others have the arme, shew us the sleeve:
We in your motion turne, and you may move us.
Then gentle brother get you in againe;
Comfort my sister, cheere her, call her wife;
'Tis holy sport to be a little vaine,
When the sweet breath of flatterie conquers strife.

FIRST FOLIO VERSE NOTES:

From the 5th line to the 15th line there is a continuous argument: **See Note 2**.

The colons are important to understanding her complete argument: **See Note 3**.

There are frequent changes from 'you' to 'thee' and back again – all indicative of changing attitudes within the speech: **See Note 22**.

With each alternative line rhyming, the '-ed' ending has to be acknowledged in such words as 'managed': **See Note 7**.

The assonances are very helpful, such as 'grow so': **See Note 10**.

Make sure all the questions are acted *as* questions.

Editors change 'make us not beleeve' to 'make us but beleeve'.

Loves Labour's lost, V-2

PRINCESSE

A time me thinkes too short,
To make a world-without-end bargaine in;
No, no my Lord, your Grace is perjur'd much,
Full of deare guiltinesse, and therefore this:
If for my Love (as there is no such cause)
You will do ought, this shall you do for me.
Your oth I will not trust: but go with speed
To some forlorne and naked Hermitage,
Remote from all the pleasures of the world:
There stay, untill the twelve Celestiall Signes
Have brought about their annuall reckoning.
If this austere insociable life,
Change not your offer made in heate of blood:
If frosts, and fasts, hard lodging, and thin weeds
Nip not the gaudie blossomes of your Love,
But that it beare this triall, and last love:
Then at the expiration of the yeare,
Come challenge me, challenge me by these deserts,
And by this Virgin palme, now kissing thine,
I will be thine: and till that instant shut
My wofull selfe up in a mourning house,
Raining the teares of lamentation,
For the remembrance of my Fathers death.
If this thou do denie, let our hands part,
Neither intitled in the others hart.

FIRST FOLIO VERSE NOTES:

The first full stop is after the sixth line, with the colons and semi-colons providing the logic for the speech: **See Notes 2 & 3**.

There are several separations, that pick out the second word, 'If for', and later on 'If frosts': **See Note 20**.

During the first part of the speech he is addressed as 'you', but for the second part, there is a change to 'thou', and a rhyming couplet to end with: **See Notes 11 & 22**.

There is a run of 'if''s all through the speech: **See Note 13**.

The word 'lamentation' needs to be made into 5 syllables to keep the meter.

Measure, For Measure, II-4

ISABELLA

To whom should I complaine? Did I tell this,
Who would beleeve me? O perilous mouthes
That beare in them, one and the selfesame tongue,
Either of condemnation, or approofe,
Bidding the Law make curtsie to their will,
Hooking both right and wrong to th'appetite,
To follow as it drawes. Ile to my brother,
Though he hath falne by prompture of the blood,
Yet hath he in him such a minde of Honor,
That had he twentie heads to tender downe
On twentie bloodie blockes, hee'ld yeeld them up,
Before his sister should her bodie stoope
To such abhord pollution.
Then *Isabell* live chaste, and brother die;
'More then our Brother, is our Chastitie.
Ile tell him yet of *Angelo's* request,
And fit his minde to death, for his soules rest.

FIRST FOLIO VERSE NOTES:

This is a soliloquy: **See Note 25**.

There is a nice assonance to start with: 'To whom': **See Note 10**, and a single 'O' to work on: **See Note 12**.

In this short speech there are 3 mid-line endings, giving a great drive to the whole: **See Notes 18 & 23**.

Towards the end there is an incomplete line 'To such abhord pollution': **See Note 17**, with a nice double meaning for abhord: **See Note 15**.

The inverted commas before 'More then our Brother, is our Chastitie.' – could mean that it is a quotation? something she had heard recently? a rule of her convent?: **See Note 4**. (Editors often leave it out, making the speech more a sign of her own priggishness.)

The separations pull out certain words: 'make curtsie'; 'his soules': **See Note 20**.

The Merchant of Venice, III-2

PORTIA

I pray you tarrie, pause a day or two
Before you hazard, for in choosing wrong
I loose your companie; therefore forbeare a while,
There's something tels me (but it is not love)
I would not loose you, and you know your selfe,
Hate counsailes not in such a quallitie;
But least you should not understand me well,
And yet a maiden hath no tongue, but thought,
I would detaine you here some month or two
Before you venture for me.   I could teach you
How to choose right, but then I am forsworne,
So will I never be, so may you misse me,
But if you doe, youle make me wish a sinne,
That I had beene forsworne: Beshrow your eyes,
They have ore-lookt me and devided me,
One halfe of me is yours, the other halfe yours,
Mine owne I would say: but of mine then yours,
And so all yours; O these naughtie times
Puts bars betweene the owners and their rights.
And so though yours, not yours (prove it so)
Let Fortune goe to hell for it, not I.
I speake too long, but 'tis to peize the time,
To ich it, and to draw it out in length,
To stay you from election.

FIRST FOLIO VERSE NOTES:

There is not a full stop for 10 lines, and then it is in the middle of the line: **See Notes 2 & 18**.

The speech then goes on for another 12 lines, showing perhaps that she is talking, and talking – maybe breaking off one thought to go into another; look at the colons and semi-colons: **See Note 3**.

There is a nice single 'O' to play with: **See Note 12**.

The choice of the end words in each line really brings the speech into focus: **See Note 9**.

'ich' is the old spelling for 'eke' or draw out: **See Note 8**, and 'peize' = weigh down; retard.

The Merchant of Venice, III-2

PORTIA

You see my Lord *Bassiano* where I stand,
Such as I am; though for my selfe alone
I would not be ambitious in my wish,
To wish my selfe much better, yet for you,
I would be trebled twenty times my selfe,
A thousand times more faire, ten thousand times
More rich, that onely to stand high in your account,
I might in vertues, beauties, livings, friends,
Exceed account: but the full summe of me
Is sum of nothing: which to terme in grosse,
Is an unlessoned girle, unschool'd, unpractiz'd,
Happy in this, she is not yet so old
But she may learne: happier then this,
Shee is not bred so dull but she can learne;
Happiest of all, is that her gentle spirit
Commits it selfe to yours to be directed,
As from her Lord, her Governour, her King.
My selfe, and what is mine, to you and yours
Is now converted.   But now I was the Lord
Of this faire mansion, master of my servants,
Queene ore my selfe: and even now, but now,
This house, these servants, and this same my selfe
Are yours, my Lord, I give them with this ring,
Which when you part from, loose, or give away,
Let it presage the ruine of your love,
And be my vantage to exclaime on you.

FIRST FOLIO VERSE NOTES:

The start of the speech is *not* 'You see me Lord Bassanio' as editors change it to, and so the actress can get the full value of a hesitant, awkward first line: **See Note 4**.

The spelling of his name as Bassiano could be a printer's error – but it also could be the way she pronounces his name at this time: **See Note 8**.

The first 17 lines are all one argument, and that is in itself an acting note: **See Note 2**.

The build on 'happy/happier/happiest' is a good clue: **See Note 13**.

The separations 'these servants' 'this same' pull the speech onto a different tack: **See Note 20**.

The Merchant of Venice, IV-1

PORTIA

The quality of mercy is not strain'd,
It droppeth as the gentle raine from heaven
Upon the place beneath.   It is twice blest,
It blesseth him that gives, and him that takes,
'Tis mightiest in the mightiest, it becomes
The throned Monarch better then his Crowne.
His Scepter shewes the force of temporall power,
The attribute to awe and Majestie,
Wherein doth sit the dread and feare of Kings:
But mercy is above this sceptred sway,
It is enthroned in the hearts of Kings,
It is an attribute to God himselfe;
And earthly power doth then shew likest Gods
When mercie seasons Justice.   Therefore Jew,
Though Justice be thy plea, consider this,
That in the course of Justice, none of us
Should see salvation: we do pray for mercie,
And that same prayer, doth teach us all to render
The deeds of mercie.   I have spoke thus much
To mittigate the justice of thy plea:
Which if thou follow, this strict course of Venice
Must needes give sentence 'gainst the Merchant there.

FIRST FOLIO VERSE NOTES:

The capitalised words in this speech are not the ones expected ('mercy' perhaps?), but all those to do with kingship and Christianity – the two elements of life in Venice that Shylocke does not have access to: **See Note 5**.

It has already been established that she knows his name is Shylocke, and addressing him as 'Jew' was then, as now, an insult: **See Notes 22 & 26**.

The alliterative build of 'mercy/mightiest/Monarch/Majestie/must/Merchant' shows where the speech is heading, and perhaps that it is not the simple plea that many make it: **See Note 10**.

The 3 mid-line endings certainly show the drive in the speech: **See Note 18**, and the colons and semi-colons help refine the argument: **See Note 3**.

'strain'd' = constrained; compelled.

A Midsommer Nights Dreame, I-1

HELENA

How happy some, ore othersome can be?
Through *Athens* I am thought as faire as she.
But what of that?   *Demetrius* thinkes not so:
He will not know, what all, but he doth know,
And as hee erres, doting on *Hermias* eyes;
So I, admiring of his qualities:
Things base and vilde, holding no quantity,
Love can transpose to forme and dignity,
Love lookes not with the eyes, but with the minde,
And therefore is wing'd *Cupid* painted blinde.
Nor hath loves minde of any judgement taste:
Wings and no eyes, figure, unheedy haste.
And therefore is Love said to be a childe,
Because in choise he is often beguil'd,
As waggish boyes in game themselves forsweare;
So the boy Love is perjur'd every where.
For ere *Demetrius* lookt on *Hermias* eyne,
He hail'd downe oathes that he was onely mine.
And when this Haile some heat from *Hermia* felt,
So he dissolv'd, and showres of oathes did melt,
I will goe tell him of faire *Hermias* flight:
Then to the wood will he, to morrow night
Pursue her; and for his intelligence,
If I have thankes, it is a deere expence:
But heerein meane I to enrich my paine,
To have his sight thither, and backe againe.

FIRST FOLIO VERSE NOTES:

This is a soliloquy: **See Note 25**.

Starting with '*Demetrius* thinks not so' there is no break in the argument for 8 lines: **See Note 2**. The next thought starts with 'Nor' – a sudden decision to extend the argument?

The last chunk is all one thought starting 'And when this Haile' – so speaking of Hermia leads to feelings not of revenge, but of helping Hermia marry Demetrius by alerting him to her flight – 'enrich my paine' indeed: **See Note 4**.

The alliterations of 'Haile/heat/*Hermia*' point up her attitude to Hermia: **See Note 10**.

The spelling of 'hee' is interesting: **See Note 6**.

The speech is made up of rhyming couplets: **See Note 11**.

'ore' = o're (over).

A Midsommer Nights Dreame, II-1

TYTANIA

These are the forgeries of jealousie,
And never since the middle Summers spring
Met we on hil, in dale, forrest, or mead,
By paved fountaine, or by rushie brooke,
Or in the beached margent of the sea,
To dance our ringlets to the whistling Winde,
But with thy braules thou hast disturb'd our sport.
Therefore the Windes, piping to us in vaine,
As in revenge, have suck'd up from the sea
Contagious fogges: Which falling in the Land,
Have everie petty River made so proud,
That they have over-borne their Continents.
The Oxe hath therefore stretch'd his yoake in vaine,
The Ploughman lost his sweat, and the greene Corne
Hath rotted, ere his youth attain'd a beard:
The fold stands empty in the drowned field,
And Crowes are fatted with the murrion flocke,
The nine mens Morris is fild up with mud,
And the queint Mazes in the wanton greene,
For lacke of tread are undistinguishable.
The humane mortals want their winter heere,
No night is now with hymne or caroll blest;
Therefore the Moone (the governesse of floods)
Pale in her anger, washes all the aire;
That Rheumaticke diseases doe abound.
And through this distemperature, we see
The seasons alter; hoared headed frosts
Fall in the fresh lap of the crimson Rose,
And on old *Hyems* chinne and Icie crowne,
An odorous Chaplet of sweet Sommer buds
Is as in mockry set. The Spring, the Sommer,
The childing Autumne, angry Winter change

Their wonted Liveries, and the mazed world,
By their increase, now knowes not which is which;
And this same progeny of evills,
Comes from our debate, from our dissention,
We are their parents and originall.

FIRST FOLIO VERSE NOTES:

The first line is not a complete thought – it is the opening up of a complex argument: **See Note 2**.

The mid-line ending towards the end gives momentum to the finish: **See Note 18**.

Be careful to keep the '-ed' endings, such as 'paved', 'beached' and 'drowned': **See Note 7**.

A lot of the expressions used in this speech have sexual imagery stitched into them, and there are many of them: **See Notes 15 & 23**; remember that a ploughman does not just plough the land.

At the end, the separation in 'this same' gives a punch to the end: **See Note 20**.

Many editors change Hyems 'chinne' to 'thin', but this image works just fine.

'pelting' = paltry.

A Midsommer Nights Dreame, III-2

PUCKE

My Mistris with a monster is in love,
Neere to her close and consecrated bower,
While she was in her dull and sleeping hower,
A crew of patches, rude Mechanicals,
That worke for bread upon *Athenian* stals,
Were met together to rehearse a Play,
Intended for great *Theseus* nuptiall day:
The shallowest thick-skin of that barren sort,
Who *Piramus* presented, in their sport,
Forsooke his Scene, and entred in a brake,
When I did him at this advantage take,
An Asses nole I fixed on his head.
Anon his *Thisbie* must be answered,
And forth my Mimmick comes: when they him spie,
As Wilde-geese, that the creeping Fowler eye,
Or russed-pated choughes, many in sort
(Rising and cawing at the guns report)
Sever themselves, and madly sweepe the skye:
So at his sight, away his fellowes flye,
And at our stampe, here ore and ore one fals;
He murther cries, and helpe from *Athens* cals.
Their sense thus weake, lost with their fears thus strong,
Made senselesse things begin to do them wrong.
For briars and thornes at their apparell snatch,
Some sleeves, some hats, from yeelders all things catch,
I led them on in this distracted feare,
And left sweete *Piramus* translated there:
When in that moment (so it came to passe)
Tytania waked, and straightway lov'd an Asse.

FIRST FOLIO VERSE NOTES:

This piece starts with a 12 line thought: **See Note 2**, and the length of the subsequent argument shows that Pucke is intent on spinning out her answer to the simple question given in order to highlight her own cleverness: **See Note 21**.

The speech starts with some good alliterations 'My/ Mistris/monster': **See Note 10**.

The speech is a good candidate for illustration: **See Note 24**.

The mention of rehearsal in the speech confuses some people; this is after all an amateur group that is being talked about, and all through history they have rehearsed, sometimes for months. Professional actors have often – for financial reasons – been given little or no rehearsal.

'russed-pated choughes' = grey-headed jackdaws.

A Midsommer Nights Dreame, III-2

HELENA

Loe, she is one of this confederacy,
Now I perceive they have conjoyn'd all three,
To fashion this false sport in spight of me.
Injurious Hermia, most ungratefull maid,
Have you conspir'd, have you with these contriv'd
To baite me, with this foule derision?
Is all the counsell that we two have shar'd,
The sisters vowes, the houres that we have spent,
When wee have chid the hasty footed time,
For parting us; O, is all forgot?
All schooledaies friendship, child-hood innocence?
We Hermia, like two Artificiall gods,
Have with our needles, created both one flower,
Both on one sampler, sitting on one cushion,
Both warbling of one song, both in one key;
As if our hands, our sides, voices, and mindes
Had beene incorporate.   So we grew together,
Like to a double cherry, seeming parted,
But yet a union in partition,
Two lovely berries molded on one stem,
So with two seeming bodies, but one heart,
Two of the first life coats in Heraldry,
Due but to one and crowned with one crest.
And will you rent our ancient love asunder,
To joyne with men in scorning your poore friend?
It is not friendly, 'tis not maidenly.
Our sexe as well as I, may chide you for it,
Though I alone doe feel the injurie.

FIRST FOLIO VERSE NOTES:

This starts as a soliloquy, and then after 3 lines she addresses the others: **See Note 25**.

There is a good separation 'false sport' at the beginning: **See Note 20**.

The repetition of all the 'two's' and 'one's' needs only to be acknowledged to get the fun in the speech: **See Note 13**.

The sudden spelling 'wee' shows the intensity of Helena's argument: **See Note 6**, and the single 'O' is a useful guide: **See Note 12**.

In the middle of the tirade, the mid-line ending gives it impetus: **See Note 18**.

Editors change 'first life coats' to 'first, like coats'.

'Loe' = look.

A Midsommer Nights Dreame, V-2

PUCKE

Now the hungry Lyons rores,
And the Wolfe beholds the Moone:
Whilest the heavy ploughman snores,
All with weary taske fore-done.
Now the wasted brands doe glow,
Whil'st the scritch-owle, scritching loud,
Puts the wretch that lies in woe,
In remembrance of a shrowd.
Now it is the time of night,
That the graves, all gaping wide,
Every one lets forth his spright,
In the Church-way paths to glide.
And we Fairies, that do runne,
By the triple *Hecates* teame,
From the presence of the Sunne,
Following darkenesse like a dreame,
Now are frollicke; not a Mouse
Shall disturbe this hallowed house.
I am sent with broome before,
To sweep the dust behinde the doore.

If we shadowes have offended,
Thinke but this (and all is mended)
That you have but slumbred heere,
While these visions did appeare.
And this weake and idle theame,
No more yeelding but a dreame,
Gentles, doe not reprehend.
If you pardon, we will mend.
And as I am an honest *Pucke*,
If we have unearned lucke,

Now to scape the Serpents tongue,
We will make amends ere long:
Else the *Pucke* a lyar call.
So good night unto you all.
Give me your hands, if we be friends,
And *Robin* shall restore amends.

FIRST FOLIO VERSE NOTES:

These speeches are soliloquies: **See Note 25**.

They are not in iambic pentameters, so will need to be approached in a different way: **See Note 19**.

In the first half, the reference to a ploughman is not an innocent country item, but also a bawdy reference to newly married couples: **See Note 15**.

The repetition of 'Now' gives a shape and drive to the speech: **See Note 13**.

The speech has alternatively rhyming lines.

In the second half, it is all in rhyming couplets: **See Note 11**.

It is interesting to see that she refers to herself first as '*Pucke*' and then as '*Robin*': **See Note 22**.

The punctuation is not as expected, and leads to an interesting theatricality: **See Note 4**.

The first half is spoken by Pucke before the final entrance of Oberon and Tytania; the second half is the epilogue to the play.

KATE

Fie, fie, unknit that thretaning unkinde brow,
And dart not scornefull glances from those eies,
To wound thy Lord, thy King, thy Governour.
It blots thy beautie, as frosts doe bite the Meads,
Confounds thy fame, as whirlewinds shake faire budds,
And in no sence is meete or amiable.
A woman mov'd, is like a fountaine troubled,
Muddie, ill seeming, thicke, bereft of beautie,
And while it is so, none so dry or thirstie
Will daigne to sip, or touch one drop of it.
Thy husband is thy Lord, thy life, thy keeper,
Thy head, thy soveraigne: One that cares for thee,
And for thy maintenance. Commits his body
To painfull labour, both by sea and land:
To watch the night in stormes, the day in cold,
Whil'st thou ly'st warme at home, secure and safe,
And craves no other tribute at thy hands,
But love, faire lookes, and true obedience;
Too little payment for so great a debt.
Such dutie as the subject owes the Prince,
Even such a woman oweth to her husband:
And when she is froward, peevish, sullen, sowre,
And not obedient to his honest will,
What is she but a foule contending Rebell,
And gracelesse Traitor to her loving Lord?
I am asham'd that women are so simple,
To offer warre, where they should kneele for peace:
Or seeke for rule, supremacie, and sway,
When they are bound to serve, love, and obay.
Why are our bodies soft, and weake, and smooth,
Unapt to toyle and trouble in the world,
But that our soft conditions, and our harts,

Should well agree with our externall parts?
Come, come, you froward and unable wormes,
My minde hath bin as bigge as one of yours,
My heart as great, my reason haplie more,
To bandie word for word, and frowne for frowne;
But now I see our Launces are but strawes:
Our strength as weake, our weakenesse past compare,
That seeming to be most, which we indeed least are.
Then vale your stomackes, for it is no boote,
And place your hands below your husbands foote:
In token of which dutie, if he please,
My hand is readie, may it do him ease.

FIRST FOLIO VERSE NOTES:

The list at the beginning: 'Lord/King/Governour' is illogical, as is the later list of 'Lord/life/keeper/head/soveraigne', and are an indication of the sincerity of the speech: **See Note 4**.

The speech is also packed with complex metaphors and similes, giving an indication as to the attitude behind the speech: **See Note 21**.

There are also a lot of assonances and alliterations: **See Note 10**; giving acting insights as to the tone of the whole speech.

The punctuation may seem illogical, but it adds to an understanding of how to act it: **See Note 4**.

After starting off addressing them as 'thy', she switches to 'you' for the end: **See Note 22**.

Acting the images in the speech show that she is ready with her hand, not that it actually is underfoot: **See Note 24**.

Troylus and Cressida, Prologue

PROLOGUE

In Troy there lyes the Scene: From Iles of Greece
The Princes Orgillous, their high blood chaf'd
Have to the Port of Athens sent their shippes
Fraught with the ministers and instruments
Of cruell Warre: Sixty and nine that wore
Their Crownets Regall, from th'Athenian bay
Put forth toward Phrygia, and their vow is made
To ransacke Troy, within whose strong emures
The ravish'd *Helen*, *Menelaus* Queene,
With wanton *Paris* sleepes, and that's the Quarrell.
To *Tenedos* they come,
And the deepe-drawing Barke do there disgorge
Their warlike frautage: now on Dardan Plaines
The fresh and yet unbruised Greekes do pitch
Their brave Pavillions. *Priams* six-gated City,
Dardan and *Timbria*, *Helias*, *Chetas*, *Trojen*,
And *Antenonidus* with massie Staples
And corresponsive and fulfilling Bolts
Stirre up the Sonnes of Troy.
Now Expectation tickling skittish spirits,
On one and other side, Trojan and Greeke,
Sets all on hazard.   And hither am I come,
A Prologue arm'd, but not in confidence
Of Authors pen, or Actors voyce; but suited
In like conditions, as our Argument;
To tell you (faire Beholders) that our Play
Leapes ore the vaunt and firstlings of those broyles,
Beginning in the middle: starting thence away,
To what may be digested in a Play:
Like, or finde fault, do as your pleasures are,
Now good, or bad, 'tis but the chance of Warre.

FIRST FOLIO VERSE NOTES:

This is a soliloquy: **See Note 25**.

The first 10 lines are all one thought leading to 'that's the Quarrell': **See Note 2**; and this is followed by a half-line: **See Note 17**. The next chunk of thought also ends with a half-line.

There are 2 half lines, with subsequent opportunities for pauses/stage business: **See Note 17**.

A lot of good capitals are to be acknowledged: **See Note 5**.

Keep the meter by defining words like 'chaf'd' and 'unbruised': **See Note 7**.

'Now Expectation tickling skittish spirits,' has both alliteration and assonance: **See Note 10**, leading up to a mid-line ending: **See Note 18**.

The whole speech ends with a rhyming couplet, remembering that 'Warre' very much rhymed with 'are' in Elizabethan days: **See Note 11**.

Some editors change 'Stirre up' to 'Sperr up' (sperr = lock).

Troylus and Cressida, I-2

CRESSIDA

By the same token you you are a Bawd.

EXIT PANDARUS.

Words, vowes, gifts, teares, and loves full sacrifice,
He offers in anothers enterprise:
But more in *Troylus* thousand fold I see,
Then in the glasse of *Pandar's* praise may be;
Yet hold I off.   Women are Angels wooing,
Things won are done, joyes soule lyes in the dooing:
That she belov'd, knowes nought, that knowes not this;
Men prize the thing ungain'd, more then it is.
That she was never yet, that ever knew
Love got so sweet, as when desire did sue:
Therefore this maxime out of love I teach;
'*Atchievement, is command;   ungain'd, beseech.*
That though my hearts Contents firme love doth beare,
Nothing of that shall from mine eyes appeare.

FIRST FOLIO VERSE NOTES:

The first thought after Pandarus' exit continues to the 6th line and 'Yet hold I off': **See Note 2**.

The next thought starts mid-line, with a consequent flourish: **See Note 18**.

The words in Italics are a quotation or saying: **See Note 5**, and the specific words in capitals are helpful as usual.

Some of the lines are difficult to say with their assonances 'won/done' and separations 'joyes soule' – and this is the acting note: **See Note 26**.

The whole is a series of rhyming couplets: **See Note 11**.

Twelfe Night, Or what you will, I-5

OLIVIA

What is your Parentage?
Above my fortunes, yet my state is well;
I am a Gentleman.   Ile be sworne thou art,
Thy tongue, thy face, thy limbes, actions, and spirit,
Do give thee five-fold blazon: not too fast: soft, soft,
Unlesse the Master were the man.   How now?
Even so quickly may one catch the plague?
Me thinkes I feele this youths perfections
With an invisible, and subtle stealth
To creepe in at mine eyes.   Well, let it be.
What hoa, *Malvolio*.

Run after that same peevish Messenger
The Countes man: he left this Ring behinde him
Would I, or not: tell him, Ile none of it.
Desire him not to flatter with his Lord,
Nor hold him up with hopes, I am not for him:
If that the youth will come this way to morrow,
Ile give him reasons for't: hie thee *Malvolio*.
I do I know not what, and feare to finde
Mine eye too great a flatterer for my minde:
Fate, shew thy force, our selves we do not owe,
What is decreed, must be: and be this so.

FIRST FOLIO VERSE NOTES:

The gaps are where Malvolio her Steward comes, gets his instructions, and then goes.

In the first part, the mid-line endings show her intensity: **See Note 18**.

The direction her list goes in: 'tongue/face/limbes/actions/ spirit' is also fascinating: **See Notes 14 and 15**.

In the second part, be careful not to put a full stop at the end of 'not for him', since the continuing thought shows what she is really after: **See Note 2**.

The final two rhyming couplets give full force to her feelings: **See Note 11**, as well as the powerful alliterations of 'feare/finde/flatterer/fate/force: **See Note 10**.

'Countes' = County's.

Twelfe Night, Or what you will, II-2

VIOLA

I left no Ring with her: what meanes this Lady?
Fortune forbid my out-side have not charm'd her:
She made good view of me, indeed so much,
That me thought her eyes had lost her tongue,
For she did speake in starts distractedly.
She loves me sure, the cunning of her passion
Invites me in this churlish messenger:
None of my Lords Ring?   Why he sent her none;
I am the man, if it be so, as tis,
Poore Lady, she were better love a dreame:
Disguise, I see thou art a wickednesse,
Wherein the pregnant enemie does much.
How easie is it, for the proper false
In womens waxen hearts to set their formes:
Alas, O frailtie is the cause, not wee,
For such as we are made, if such we bee:
How will this fadge?   My master loves her deerely,
And I (poore monster) fond as much on him:
And she (mistaken) seemes to dote on me:
What will become of this?   As I am man,
My state is desperate for my maisters love:
As I am woman (now alas the day)
What thriftlesse sighes shall poore *Olivia* breath?
O time, thou must untangle this, not I,
It is too hard a knot for me t'unty.

FIRST FOLIO VERSE NOTES:

This is a soliloquy, and is to be shared with the audience: **See Note 25**.

The thoughts and arguments do not always end where expected, as 'better love a dreame' is *not* the end of that section; this leads to a more interesting interpretation: **See Note 4**.

Right in the middle of the speech is an unexpected rhyming couplet 'wee/bee', and this must be theatricalized: **See Note 11**, as well as noticing their spelling: **See Note 6**.

There are 2 single 'O''s to play with: **See Note 12**.

There is word play 'not/knot' at the end: **See Note 15**.

Editors change 'O frailtie' to 'our frailtie'; and 'For such as we are made, if such we bee:' to 'For such as we are made of, such we be.'

'fadge' = work out.

The Two Gentlemen of Verona, I-2

JULIA

Now (by my modesty) a goodly Broker:
Dare you presume to harbour wanton lines?
To whisper, and conspire against my youth?
Now trust me, 'tis an office of great worth,
And you an officer fit for the place:
There: take the paper: see it be return'd,
Or else returne no more into my sight.

Will ye be gon?

And yet I would I had ore-look'd the Letter;
It were a shame to call her backe againe,
And pray her to a fault, for which I chid her.
What 'foole is she, that knowes I am a Maid,
And would not force the letter to my view?
Since Maides, in modesty, say no, to that,
Which they would have the profferer construe, I.
Fie, fie: how way-ward is this foolish love;
That (like a testie Babe) will scratch the Nurse,
And presently, all humbled kisse the Rod?
How churlishly, I chid *Lucetta* hence,
When willingly, I would have had her here?
How angerly I taught my brow to frowne,
When inward joy enforc'd my heart to smile?
My pennance is, to call *Lucetta* backe
And aske remission, for my folly past.
What hoe: *Lucetta*.

FIRST FOLIO VERSE NOTES:

The first chunk is to Lucetta her maid, and the second is a soliloquy: **See Note 25**.

There are brackets to put into the acting: **See Note 16**.

The speech also has some nice alliterations and assonances in: 'I/Fie'; 'churlishly/chid'; 'when/willingly': **See Note 10**.

Remember that 'I' can also be 'Aye': **See Note 8**.

Make sure the questions are acted *as* questions.

The gaps are where Lucetta has a short reply, and where she exits.

The Two Gentlemen of Verona, I-2

JULIA

This babble shall not henceforth trouble me;
Here is a coile with protestation:
Goe, get you gone: and let the papers lye:
You would be fingring them, to anger me.

Nay, would I were so angred with the same:
Oh hatefull hands, to teare such loving words;
Injurious Waspes, to feede on such sweet hony,
And kill the Bees that yeelde it, with your stings;
Ile kisse each severall paper, for amends:
Looke, here is writ, kinde *Julia*: unkinde *Julia*,
As in revenge of thy ingratitude,
I throw thy name against the bruzing-stones,
Trampling contemptuously on thy disdaine.
And here is writ, *Love wounded Protheus*.
Poore wounded name: my bosome, as a bed,
Shall lodge thee till thy wound be throughly heal'd;
And thus I search it with a soveraigne kisse.
But twice, or thrice, was *Protheus* written downe:
Be calme (good winde) blow not a word away,
Till I have found each letter, in the Letter,
Except mine own name: That, some whirle-winde beare
Unto a ragged, fearefull, hanging Rocke,
And throw it thence into the raging Sea.
Loe, here in one line is his name twice writ:
Poore forlorne Protheus, passionate Protheus:
To the sweet Julia: that ile teare away:
And yet I will not, sith so prettily
He couples it, to his complaining Names;
Thus will I fold them, one upon another;
Now kisse, embrace, contend, doe what you will.

FIRST FOLIO VERSE NOTES:

The first chunk is to the other person, the second (after the gap where the other person exits) is a soliloquy: **See Note 25**.

She addresses the other person as 'you', but the pieces of paper as 'thee' – except in the final line when she is encouraging the paper to be bawdy: **See Note 22**.

There are plenty of alliterations and assonances to use: 'hateful/hands'; 'feede/sweet': **See Note 10**.

The words in italics are those she reads from the paper: **See Note 5**.

There is a constant veering from the simplicity of a 'Looke, here is writ' to the complexity of images of the raging sea: **See Note 21**.

The Two Gentlemen of Verona, IV-4

JULIA

And she shall thanke you for't, if ere you know her.
A vertuous gentlewoman, milde, and beautifull.
I hope my Masters suit will be but cold,
Since she respects my Mistris love so much.
Alas, how love can trifle with it selfe:
Here is her Picture: let me see, I thinke
If I had such a Tyre, this face of mine
Were full as lovely, as is this of hers;
And yet the Painter flatter'd her a little,
Unlesse I flatter with my selfe too much.
Her haire is *Aburne*, mine is perfect *Yellow*;
If that be all the difference in his love,
Ile get me such a coulour'd Perrywig:
Her eyes are grey as glasse, and so are mine:
I, but her fore-head's low, and mine's as high:
What should it be that he respects in her,
But I can make respective in my selfe?
If this fond Love, were not a blinded god.
Come shadow, come, and take this shadow up,
For 'tis thy rivall: O thou sencelesse forme,
Thou shalt be worship'd, kiss'd, lov'd, and ador'd;
And were there sence in his Idolatry,
My substance should be statue in thy stead.
Ile use thee kindly, for thy Mistris sake
That us'd me so: or else by *Jove*, I vow,
I should have scratch'd out your unseeing eyes,
To make my Master out of love with thee.

FIRST FOLIO VERSE NOTES:

There are an unusually large amount of full stops in the first half of the speech: **See Note 4**.

Remember that 'I' can also be 'Aye': **See Note 8**.

There is a nice 'O' to be used: **See Note 12**.

In the penultimate line there is a sudden 'your' surrounded by 'thees' – showing a sudden change of attitude or mood: **See Note 22**.

The list 'worship'd/kiss'd/lov'd/ador'd' goes in an interesting order: **See Note 14**.

There are good separations to be used, such as 'Masters suit' and 'Mistris sake': **See Note 20**.

The Tragedie of Anthonie, and Cleopatra, I-5

CLEOPATRA

Oh *Charmion*:
Where think'st thou he is now?   Stands he, or sits he?
Or does he walke?   Or is he on his Horse?
Oh happy horse to beare the weight of *Anthony*!
Do bravely Horse, for wot'st thou whom thou moov'st,
The demy *Atlas* of this Earth, the Arme
And Burganet of men.   Hee's speaking now,
Or murmuring, where's my Serpent of old Nyle,
(For so he cals me:) Now I feede my selfe
With most delicious poyson.   Thinke on me
That am with Phœbus amorous pinches blacke,
And wrinkled deepe in time.   Broad-fronted *Cæsar*,
When thou was't heere above the ground, I was
A morsell for a Monarke: and great *Pompey*
Would stand and make his eyes grow in my brow,
There would he anchor his Aspect, and dye
With looking on his life.

FIRST FOLIO VERSE NOTES:

The speech has 5 mid-line endings, that will give a pace to the proceedings: **See Note 18**.

There are many erotic images in the text, culminating in the word 'dye' that was both the 'little death' of orgasm as well as the more traditional interpretation: **See Note 15**.

The languid assonances: 'am/amorous/blacke' add to the feeling of the piece: **See Note 10**.

The capitalized words in the speech are revealing: **See Note 5**.

Choosing the end words, such as 'Arme; selfe; me; was; dye' gives a particular meaning to those lines: **See Note 9**.

'Burganet' = helmet.

The Tragedie of Anthonie, and Cleopatra, V-2

CLEOPATRA

I dreampt there was an Emperor *Anthony*.
Oh such another sleepe, that I might see
But such another man.

His face was as the Heav'ns, and therein stucke
A Sunne and Moone, which kept their course, and lighted
The little o'th'earth.

His legges bestrid the Ocean, his rear'd arme
Crested the world: His voyce was propertied
As all the tuned Spheres, and that to Friends:
But when he meant to quaile, and shake the Orbe,
He was as ratling Thunder.   For his Bounty,
There was no winter in't.   An *Anthony* it was,
That grew the more by reaping: His delights
Were Dolphin-like, they shew'd his backe above
The Element they liv'd in: In his Livery
Walk'd Crownes and Crownets: Realmes and Islands were
As plates dropt from his pocket.

Thinke you there was, or might be such a man
As this I dreampt of?

You Lye up to the hearing of the Gods:
But if there be, nor ever were one such
It's past the size of dreaming: Nature wants stuffe
To vie strange formes with fancie, yet t'imagine
An *Anthony* were Natures peece, 'gainst Fancie,
Condemning shadowes quite.

FIRST FOLIO VERSE NOTES:

In the main body of the speech, there are only mid-line endings, driving all before it: **See Notes 2 & 18**.

The sexual imagery is explicit – remembering the motion of dolphins in the sea: **See Note 15**.

The sense of the speech is helped by clearly choosing the end words in each verse line: **See Note 9**.

There are some nice sparations towards the end: 'wants stuffe; yet t'imagine': **See Note 20**.

Editors have been known to change the text from 'An *Anthony* it was,' to 'an autumn it was'. They also change 'The little o'th'earth.' to 'The little O, th'earth.', influenced by anything circular (such as the Globe) being known as an O.

The gaps are where there are a few words from Dolabella.

The Tragedie of Anthonie, and Cleopatra, V-2

CLEOPATRA

Give me my Robe, put on my Crowne, I have
Immortall longings in me. Now no more
The juyce of Egypts Grape shall moyst this lip.
Yare, yare, good *Iras*; quicke: Me thinkes I heare
Anthony call: I see him rowse himselfe
To praise my Noble Act.   I heare him mock
The lucke of *Cæsar*, which the Gods give men
To excuse their after wrath.   Husband, I come:
Now to that name, my Courage prove my Title.
I am Fire, and Ayre; my other Elements
I give to baser life.   So, have you done?
Come then, and take the last warmth of my Lippes.
Farewell kinde *Charmian*, *Iras*, long farewell.
Have I the Aspicke in my lippes?   Dost fall?
If thou, and Nature can so gently part,
The stroke of death is as a Lovers pinch,
Which hurts, and is desir'd.   Dost thou lye still?
If thus thou vanishest, thou tell'st the world,
It is not worth leave-taking.

This proves me base:
If she first meete the Curled *Anthony*,
Hee'l make demand of her, and spend that kisse
Which is my heaven to have.   Come thou mortal wretch,
With thy sharpe teeth this knot intrinsicate,
Of life at once untye: Poore venemous Foole,
Be angry, and dispatch.   Oh could'st thou speake,
That I might heare thee call great *Caesar* Asse,
                              unpolicied.

Peace, peace:
Dost thou not see my Baby at my breast,
That suckes the Nurse asleep.

As sweet as Balme, as soft as Ayre, as gentle.
O *Anthony*!   Nay I will take thee too.
What should I stay –

DYES.

FIRST FOLIO VERSE NOTES:

The end words of each line, especially the first one, need to be chosen and used: **See Note 9**.

The thoughts end in mid-line 9 times – but also at the end of a line 8 times – so there is a clear pattern to act the speech with: **See Note 18**.

She calls him '*Anthony*' at first, but then 'Husband': **See Note 22**, and the 'you' to her maids is tempered to 'thou' when death strikes Iras down. The asps (snakes) are 'thou'.

The first part of the name Charmian is pronounced like the first part of the word charming: **See Note 6**.

There is one very long line starting 'That I might heare' **See Note 17**.

The gaps are where Charmian speaks short lines.

'Yare' = quick; nimble.

The Tragedy of Coriolanus, V-3

VOLUMNIA

Should we be silent and not speak, our Raiment
And state of Bodies would bewray what life
We have led since thy Exile.   Thinke with thy selfe,
How more unforunate then all living women
Are we come hither; since that thy sight, which should
Make our eies flow with joy, harts dance with comforts,
Constraines them weepe, and shake with feare and
sorow,
Making the Mother, wife, and Childe to see,
The Sonne, the Husband, and the Father tearing
His Countries Bowels out; and to poore we
Thine enmities most capitall: Thou barr'st us
Our prayers to the Gods, which is a comfort
That all but we enjoy.   For how can we?
Alas! how can we, for our Country pray?
Whereto we are bound, together with thy victory:
Whereto we are bound: Alacke, or we must loose
The Countrie our deere Nurse, or else thy person
Our comfort in the Country.   We must finde
An evident Calamity, though we had
Our wish, which side should win.   For either thou
Must as a Forraine Recreant be led
With Manacles through our streets, or else
Triumphantly treade on thy Countries ruine,
And beare the Palme, for having bravely shed
Thy Wife and Childrens blood: For my selfe, Sonne,
I purpose not to waite on Fortune, till
These warres determine: If I cannot perswade thee,
Rather to shew a Noble grace to both parts,
Then seeke the end of one; thou shalt no sooner
March to assault thy Country, then to treade
(Trust too't, thou shalt not) on thy Mothers wombe
That brought thee to this world.

FIRST FOLIO VERSE NOTES:

The speech is full of feminine endings, as well as very carefully chosen words to end each verse line: **See Note 9**.

The capitalized words help a lot: **See Note 5**.

The long thoughts all ending in the middle of a line give shape to the whole speech: **See Notes 2 & 18 & 23**.

The list 'Sonne/Husband/Father' is a precise insight into her priorities: **See Note 14**.

The word Country is repeated 6 times, and that is significant: **See Note 13**, and 'bewray' = reveal.

The Tragedy of Coriolanus, V-3

VOLUMNIA

Nay, go not from us thus:
If it were so, that our request did tend
To save the Romanes, thereby to destroy
The Volces whom you serve, you might condemne us
As poysonous of your Honour.   No, our suite
Is that you reconcile them: While the Volces
May say, this mercy we have shew'd: the Romanes,
This we receiv'd, and each in either side
Give the All-haile to thee, and cry be Blest
For making up this peace.   Thou know'st (great Sonne)
The end of Warres uncertaine: but this certaine,
That if thou conquer Rome, the benefit
Which thou shalt thereby reape, is such a name
Whose repetition will be dogg'd with Curses:
Whose Chronicle thus writ, The man was Noble,
But with his last Attempt, he wip'd it out:
Destroy'd his Country, and his name remaines
To th'insuing Age, abhorr'd.   Speake to me Son:
Thou hast affected the five straines of Honor,
To imitate the graces of the Gods.
To teare with Thunder the wide Cheekes a'th'Ayre,
And yet to change thy Sulphure with a Boult
That should but rive an Oake.   Why do'st not speake?
Think'st thou it Honourable for a Nobleman
Still to remember wrongs?   Daughter, speake you:
He cares not for your weeping.   Speake thou Boy,
Perhaps thy childishnesse will move him more
Then can our Reasons.   There's no man in the world
More bound to's Mother, yet heere he let's me prate
Like one i'th'Stockes.   Thou hast never in thy life,
Shew'd thy deere Mother any curtesie,
When she (poore Hen) fond of no second brood,
Ha's clock'd thee to the Warres: and safelie home
Loden with Honor.   Say my Request's unjust,
And spurne me backe: But, if it be not so
Thou art not honest, and the Gods will plague thee

That thou restrain'st from me the Duty, which
To a Mothers part belongs.   He turnes away:
Down Ladies: let us shame him with our knees
To his sur-name *Coriolanus* longs more pride
Then pitty to our Prayers.   Downe: an end,
This is the last.   So, we will home to Rome,
And dye among our Neighbours: Nay, behold's,
This Boy that cannot tell what he would have,
But kneeles, and holds up hands for fellowship,
Doe's reason our Petition with more strength
Then thou hast to deny't.   Come, let us go:
This Fellow had a Volcean to his Mother:
His Wife is in *Corioles*, and his Childe
Like him by chance: yet give us our dispatch:
I am husht untill our City be afire, and then Ile speak a litle.

FIRST FOLIO VERSE NOTES:

Choosing the end words and the words in capitals help the speech: **See Notes 5 & 9**.

There are 13 mid-line endings to give pace and drive to all she says: **See Note 18**. It is practically a record for a single speech, and so is a big clue as to her attitude: **See Note 23**.

The separations of 'this certaine', 'is such', and 'his sur-name' are useful in feeling her mood: **See Note 20**.

The speech is also shaped by her addressing her son as 'you' to start with, and then switching to the more intimate 'thee' later: **See Note 22**.

The last line is really long – it is an interesting change to prose: **See Note 1**.

Editors change 'five straines of Honor' to 'fine straines of Honor', and 'change thy Sulphure' to 'charge thy Sulphure'.

In the Folio the line is printed 'Down Ladies: let us shame him with him with our knees', and we have reluctantly joined with editors in omitting the superfluous 'with him'.

'longs' = belongs.

The Tragedie of Hamlet, III-1

OPHELIA

O what a Noble minde is heere o're-throwne?
The Courtiers, Soldiers, Schollers: Eye, tongue, sword,
Th'expectansie and Rose of the faire State,
The glasse of Fashion, and the mould of Forme,
Th'observ'd of all Observers, quite, quite downe.
Have I of Ladies most deject and wretched,
That suck'd the Honie of his Musicke Vowes:
Now see that Noble, and most Soveraigne Reason,
Like sweet Bels jangled out of tune, and harsh,
That unmatch'd Forme and Feature of blowne youth,
Blasted with extasie.   Oh woe is me,
T'have seene what I have seene: see what I see.

FIRST FOLIO VERSE NOTES:

The first line is stuffed with assonating words: 'O/Noble/ o're-throwne', and these are a good guide to the sincerity or not of the speech: **See Note 10**.

These elaborate vowels sounds continue through the speech – and someone expressing themselves in complicated ways is someone struggling to express a complex (not simple) feeling: **See Note 21**.

The long spelling of 'heere' is to be used: **See Note 6**.

The mid-line ending towards the end suddenly changes the mood: **See Note 18**.

The last line is stark contrast to what has gone before, but even here is the repeated word 'see': **See Note 13**.

The Tragedie of Hamlet, IV-7

GERTRUDE

There is a Willow growes aslant a Brooke,
That shewes his hore leaves in the glassie streame:
There with fantasticke Garlands did she come,
Of Crow-flowers, Nettles, Daysies, and long Purples,
That liberall Shepheards give a grosser name;
But our cold Maids doe Dead Mens Fingers call them:
There on the pendant boughes, her Coronet weeds
Clambring to hang; an envious sliver broke,
When downe the weedy Trophies, and her selfe,
Fell in the weeping Brooke, her cloathes spred wide,
And Mermaid-like, a while they bore her up,
Which time she chaunted snatches of old tunes,
As one incapable of her owne distresse,
Or like a creature Native, and indued
Unto that Element: but long it could not be,
Till that her garments, heavy with her drinke,
Pul'd the poore wretch from her melodious buy,
To muddy death.

FIRST FOLIO VERSE NOTES:

This report of an event, like many descriptive passages, does not mean that the event happened as described (and that Gertrude stood and watched Ophelia drown). Since the speech is also stuffed with bawdy meanings 'hore leaves', 'long purples', and even the first line can produce a double entendre, it would seem that she has a lot more going on than just reporting an accident: **See Notes 15 & 21 & 26**.

The whole passage is one long argument, as Gertrude describes the end of Ophelia (and in so doing, reveals to the audience how she felt about her?): **See Note 2**.

The separations of 'envious sliver', and 'cloathes spred' give a hint as to her attitude: **See Note 20**.

The speech, although complicated and full of images, ends with a simple statement: **See Note 21**.

The Tragedie of Julius Cæsar, II-1

PORTIA

Nor for yours neither.   Y'have ungently *Brutus*
Stole from my bed: and yesternight at Supper
You sodainly arose, and walk'd about,
Musing, and sighing, with your armes a-crosse:
And when I ask'd you what the matter was,
You star'd upon me, with ungentle lookes.
I urg'd you further, then you scratch'd your head,
And too impatiently stampt with your foote:
Yet I insisted, yet you answer'd not,
But with an angry wafter of your hand
Gave signe for me to leave you: So I did,
Fearing to strengthen that impatience
Which seem'd too much inkindled; and withall,
Hoping it was but an effect of Humor,
Which sometime hath his houre with every man.
It will not let you eate, nor talke, nor sleepe;
And could it worke so much upon your shape,
As it hath much prevayl'd on your Condition,
I should not know you *Brutus*.   Deare my Lord,
Make me acquainted with your cause of greefe.

FIRST FOLIO VERSE NOTES:

The speech starts with a mid-line ending, and then launches into a 6 line thought: **See Notes 2 & 18**.

The thought starts and ends with the idea 'ungentle': **See Note 13**.

The next thought is also long, ending mid-line — adding momentum and drive to the speech.

She starts by addressing him as '*Brutus*' — but ends by calling him 'my Lord': **See Note 22**.

The Tragedie of Julius Cæsar, II-1

PORTIA

Is *Brutus* sicke?   And is it Physicall
To walke unbraced, and sucke up the humours
Of the danke Morning?   What, is *Brutus* sicke?
And will he steale out of his wholsome bed
To dare the vile contagion of the Night?
And tempt the Rhewmy, and unpurged Ayre,
To adde unto his sicknesse?   No my *Brutus*,
You have some sicke Offence within your minde,
Which by the Right and Vertue of my place
I ought to know of: And upon my knees,
I charme you, by my once commended Beauty,
By all your vowes of Love, and that great Vow
Which did incorporate and make us one,
That you unfold to me, your selfe; your halfe
Why you are heavy: and what men to night
Have had resort to you: for heere have beene
Some sixe or seven, who did hide their faces
Even from darknesse.

I should not neede, if you were gentle *Brutus*.
Within the Bond of Marriage, tell me *Brutus*,
Is it excepted, I should know no Secrets
That appertaine to you?   Am I your Selfe,
But as it were in sort, or limitation?
To keepe with you at Meales, comfort your Bed,
And talke to you sometimes?   Dwell I but in the Suburbs
Of your good pleasure?   If it be no more,
Portia is *Brutus* Harlot, not his Wife.

If this were true, then should I know this secret.
I graunt I am a Woman; but withall,
A Woman that Lord *Brutus* tooke to Wife:
I graunt I am a Woman; but withall,

A Woman well reputed: *Cato*'s Daughter.
Thinke you, I am no stronger then my Sex
Being so Father'd, and so Husbanded?
Tell me your Counsels, I will not disclose 'em:
I have made strong proofe of my Constancie,
Giving my selfe a voluntary wound
Heere, in the Thigh: Can I beare that with patience,
And not my Husbands Secrets?

FIRST FOLIO VERSE NOTES:

The separations in this speech, the '*Brutus* sicke' couplings, allow the performer to choose and pick out these ideas carefully: **See Note 20**.

The first line has 5 words assonating, giving a particular edge to the start: **See Note 10**.

To keep the drive of the meter, the '-ed' endings need to be observed: **See Note 7**.

There are some nice capitalised words, that show where her priorities are: **See Note 5**.

The first part of the speech is mostly devoid of full stops, and so is a long argument rather than a series of statements: **See Note 2**.

The second part has 3 mid-line endings See Note 18; and the last part has the repetition of the word 'Woman' **See Note 13**.

The gaps are where Brutus tells her not to kneel, and that she is his dear wife.

The Suburbs were where the brothels were to be found, and the thigh was always considered to be at the top end of the leg, with consequences as to where the wound was that she had made, and what she is showing him now.

The early part of the speech is full of adjectives and images, and ends with the stark statement 'what men to night have had resort to you': **See Note 21**.

The Tragedie of Macbeth, I-5

LADY MACBETH

Give him tending,
He brings great newes.

EXIT MESSENGER.

The Raven himselfe is hoarse,
That croakes the fatall entrance of *Duncan*
Under my Battlements.   Come you Spirits,
That tend on mortall thoughts, unsex me here,
And fill me from the Crowne to the Toe, top-full
Of direst Crueltie: make thick my blood,
Stop up th'accesse, and passage to Remorse,
That no compunctious visitings of Nature
Shake my fell purpose, nor keepe peace betweene
Th'effect, and hit.   Come to my Womans Brests,
And take my Milke for Gall, you murth'ring Ministers,
Where-ever, in your sightlesse substances,
You wait on Natures Mischiefe.   Come thick Night,
And pall thee in the dunnest smoake of Hell,
That my keene Knife see not the Wound it makes,
Nor Heaven peepe through the Blanket of the darke,
To cry, hold, hold.

ENTER MACBETH.

Great Glamys, worthy Cawdor,
Greater then both, by the all-haile hereafter,
Thy Letters have transported me beyond
This ignorant present, and I feele now
The future in the instant.

FIRST FOLIO VERSE NOTES:

This is a soliloquy: **See Note 25**.

There are 3 mid-line endings, all before 'Come', which indicates that she does not make a request and wait for the answer, but (believing it is not coming?) drives on to the next request: **See Note 18**.

The progress of her requests is interesting, starting off with the most profound, and ending up with a simple request for night to come that will be fulfilled whether the spirits grant her request or no, and the repetition of 'Come' could be because in effect no-one does: **See Notes 13 & 14**.

At first, she addresses the spirits as 'you', but for her final request it is changed to 'thee': **See Note 22**.

The capitalised words pick out an interesting series of steps through the speech, that is diminished if artificial pauses and business are put in where Shakespeare has quite clearly indicated otherwise: **See Notes 5 & 17**.

Editors change 'Th'effect, and hit' to 'Th'effect, and it'.

The Tragedie of Macbeth, I-7

LADY MACBETH

Was the hope drunke,
Wherein you drest your selfe?   Hath it slept since?
And wakes it now to looke so greene, and pale,
At what it did so freely?   From this time,
Such I account thy love.   Art thou affear'd
To be the same in thine owne Act, and Valour,
As thou art in desire?   Would'st thou have that
Which thou esteem'st the Ornament of Life,
And live a Coward in thine owne Esteeme?
Letting I dare not, wait upon I would,
Like the poore Cat i'th'Addage.

What Beast was't then
That made you breake this enterprize to me?
When you durst do it, then you were a man:
And to be more then what you were, you would
Be so much more the man.   Nor time, nor place
Did then adhere, and yet you would make both:
They have made themselves, and that their fitnesse now
Do's unmake you.   I have given Sucke, and know
How tender 'tis to love the Babe that milkes me,
I would, while it was smyling in my Face,
Have pluckt my Nipple from his Bonelesse Gummes,
And dasht the Braines out, had I so sworne
As you have done to this.

FIRST FOLIO VERSE NOTES:

The capitals in the speech are useful: **See Note 5**.

The thoughts tend to end in the middle of a line — in fact there are 6 mid-line endings: **See Notes 2 & 18**.

She starts off addressing him as 'you', switches to 'thou', but she is back to 'you' for the end: **See Note 22**.

There is a nice separation 'was smyling': **See Note 20**.

Make sure all the questions are acted *as* questions. The gap is where Macbeth has a single line of disagreement.

'th'Addage' seems to be: 'The cat would eat fish, but would not wet its feet'.

The Tragedie of Othello, IV-2

DESDEMONA

Alas *Iago*,
What shall I do to win my Lord againe?
Good Friend, go to him: for by this light of Heaven,
I know not how I lost him.   Heere I kneele:
If ere my will did trespasse 'gainst his Love,
Either in discourse of thought, or actuall deed,
Or that mine Eyes, mine Eares, or any Sence
Delighted them: or any other Forme,
Or that I do not yet, and ever did,
And ever will, (though he do shake me off
To beggerly divorcement) Love him deerely,
Comfort forsweare me.   Unkindnesse may do much,
And his unkindnesse may defeat my life,
But never taynt my Love.   I cannot say Whore,
It do's abhorre me now I speake the word,
To do the Act, that might the addition earne,
Not the worlds Masse of vanitie could make me.

FIRST FOLIO VERSE NOTES:

The first mid-line ending is followed by an illustration of what to do (and so how to do it): **See Notes 18 & 24**. The next 2 thoughts also end mid-line: **See Note 23**.

The capitalized words help the intensity of the speech: **See Note 5**.

The dreadful pun between 'Whore' and 'abhorre' does not necessarily indicate a light approach; often in times of stress we make bad jokes: **See Notes 15 & 21**.

The last line is very complicated and difficult to say, and those *are* the acting clues for how to end the speech.

Editors change 'or any other Forme' to 'in any other Forme'.

The Tragedie of Othello, IV-3

ÆMILIA

Yes, a dozen: and as many to'th'vantage, as
would store the world they plaid for.
But I do thinke it is their Husbands faults
If Wives do fall: (Say, that they slacke their duties,
And powre our Treasures into forraigne laps;
Or else breake out in peevish Jealousies,
Throwing restraint upon us: Or say they strike us,
Or scant our former having in despight)
Why we have galles: and though we have some Grace,
Yet have we some Revenge.   Let Husbands know,
Their wives have sense like them: They see, and smell,
And have their Palats both for sweet, and sowre,
As Husbands have.   What is it that they do,
When they change us for others?   Is it Sport?
I thinke it is: and doth Affection breed it?
I thinke it doth.   Is't Frailty that thus erres?
It is so too.   And have not we Affections?
Desires for Sport? and Frailty, as men have?
Then let them use us well: else let them know,
The illes we do, their illes instruct us so.

FIRST FOLIO VERSE NOTES:

The first 2 lines are prose, only then does she speak in verse: **See Note 1**.

There are 6 mid-line endings, adding drive to the speech: **See Note 18**, as well as 7 question marks — make sure they are acted as questions and not statements.

A large 5 line chunk is in brackets: **See Note 16**, and again needs to be acted as such.

The capitals help in their usual way: **See Note 5**, and the punctuation of the argument is not always what you would expect: **See Note 4**.

The Tragedie of Romeo and Juliet, II-2

JULIET

Thou knowest the maske of night is on my face,
Else would a Maiden blush bepaint my cheeke,
For that which thou hast heard me speake to night,
Faine would I dwell on forme, faine, faine, denie
What I have spoke, but farewell Complement,
Doest thou Love?   I know thou wilt say I,
And I will take thy word, yet if thou swear'st,
Thou maiest prove false: at Lovers perjuries
They say *Jove* laught, oh gentle *Romeo*,
If thou dost Love, pronounce it faithfully:
Or if thou thinkest I am too quickly wonne,
Ile frowne and be perverse, and say thee nay,
So thou wilt wooe: But else not for the world.
In truth faire *Montague* I am too fond:
And therefore thou maiest thinke my behaviour light,
But trust me Gentleman, Ile prove more true,
Than those that have coying to be strange,
I should have beene more strange, I must confesse,
But that thou over heard'st ere I was ware
My true Loves passion, therefore pardon me,
And not impute this yeelding to light Love,
Which the darke night hath so discovered.

FIRST FOLIO VERSE NOTES:

The first 6 lines are one thought ending in a mid-line ending: **See Notes 2 & 18**, and the whole speech is in just 3 thoughts.

It is interesting that Juliet does not wait for an answer to 'Doest thou Love?' but charges straight on: **See Note 4**.

The use of 'I' with its several meanings, the careful choices of alliterations and assonances, make this speech deliberately clever: **See Notes 10 & 26**.

The final assonance between 'Love' and 'discovered' means the '-ed' needs to be pronounced: **See Note 7**.

Editors change 'coying' to 'more cunning', but leaving it as it is gives a nice odd-length line and hesitation to the speech: **See Note 17**.

The Tragedie of Romeo and Juliet, III-2

JULIET

Gallop apace, you fiery footed steedes,
Towards *Phœbus* lodging, such a Wagoner
As *Phæton* would whip you to the west,
And bring in Cloudie night immediately.
Spred thy close Curtaine Love-performing night,
That run-awayes eyes may wincke, and *Romeo*
Leape to these armes, untalkt of and unseene,
Lovers can see to doe their Amorous rights,
And by their owne Beauties: or if Love be blind,
It best agrees with night: come civill night,
Thou sober suted Matron all in blacke,
And learne me how to loose a winning match,
Plaid for a paire of stainlesse Maidenhoods,
Hood my unman'd blood bayting in my Cheekes,
With thy Blacke mantle, till strange Love grow bold,
Thinke true Love acted simple modestie:
Come night, come *Romeo,* come thou day in night,
For thou wilt lie upon the wings of night
Whiter then new Snow upon a Ravens backe:
Come gentle night, come loving blackebrow'd night.
Give me my *Romeo*, and when I shall die,
Take him and cut him out in little starres,
And he will make the Face of heaven so fine,
That all the world will be in Love with night,
And pay no worship to the Garish Sun.
O I have bought the Mansion of a Love,
But not possest it, and though I am sold,
Not yet enjoy'd, so tedious is this day,
As is the night before some Festivall,

To an impatient child that hath new robes
And may not weare them, O here comes my Nurse:

ENTER NURSE WITH CORDS.

And she brings newes and every tongue that speaks
But *Romeos* name, speakes heavenly eloquence:
Now Nurse, what newes? what hast thou there?
The Cords that *Romeo* bid thee fetch?

FIRST FOLIO VERSE NOTES:

The speech is a soliloquy — talking to the audience, not chatting eloquently to oneself: **See Note 25**.

The italicised words are proper names, and those in capitals need to be acknowledged: **See Note 5**.

The punctuation of the colons and semi-colons illuminate the argument she is making: **See Note 3**.

There is a lot of sexual innuendo in this speech 'Love grow bold' etc, with all those double entendres: **See Note 15**. The word 'die' in those days not only meant the end of life, but was also used for the moment of sexual ecstasy.

The clever words and complex structure in the speech does not work if it is done at a gallop — in the first line Juliet is watching the sun setting, and she takes her time (6 lines) before she even mentions Romeo's name: **See Note 21**.

When the Nurse enters, even here Juliet takes 4 lines before she finally awaits the Nurse's reply to her question: **See Note 4**.

The Tragedie of Romeo and Juliet, IV-3

JULIET

Farewell:
God knowes when we shall meete againe.
I have a faint cold feare thrills through my veines,
That almost freezes up the heate of fire:
Ile call them backe againe to comfort me.
Nurse, what should she do here?
My dismall Sceane, I needs must act alone:
Come Viall, what if this mixture do not worke at all?
Shall I be married then to morrow morning?
No, no, this shall forbid it. Lie thou there,
What if it be a poyson which the Frier
Subtilly hath ministred to have me dead,
Least in this marriage he should be dishonour'd,
Because he married me before to *Romeo*?
I feare it is, and yet me thinkes it should not,
For he hath still beene tried a holy man.
How, if when I am laid into the Tombe,
I wake before the time that *Romeo*
Come to redeeme me?   There's a fearefull point:
Shall I not then be stifled in the Vault?
To whose foule mouth no healthsome ayre breaths in,
And there die strangled ere my *Romeo* comes.
Or if I live, is it not very like,
The horrible conceit of death and night,
Together with the terror of the place,
As in a Vaulte, an ancient receptacle,
Where for these many hundred yeeres the bones
Of all my buried Auncestors are packt,
Where bloody *Tybalt*, yet but greene in earth,
Lies festring in his shrow'd, where as they say,
At some houres in the night, Spirits resort:
Alacke, alacke, is it not like that I
So early waking, what with loathsome smels,
And shrikes like Mandrakes torne out of the earth,

That living mortalls hearing them, run mad.
O if I walke, shall I not be distraught,
Invironed with all these hidious feares,
And madly play with my forefathers joynts?
And plucke the mangled *Tybalt* from his shrow'd?
And in this rage, with some great kinsmans bone,
As (with a club) dash out my desperate braines.
O looke, me thinks I see my Cozins Ghost,
Seeking out *Romeo* that did spit his body
Upon my Rapiers point: stay *Tybalt*, stay;
Romeo, Romeo, Romeo, here's drinke: I drinke to thee.

FIRST FOLIO VERSE NOTES:

This speech is done to and for the audience, and as a soliloquy is not a conversation with oneself: **See Note 25**.

The first 2 lines are incomplete, indicating business; in the same way the 6th line is an unfinished line, so stage business is indicated at this point as well: **See Note 17**.

There are 2 mid-line endings, that keep the speech driving on: **See Note 18**.

There is a progression of 'What if/How, if/Or if/O if'; and finally 'O looke,' to show the build in the speech: **See Notes 14 & 23**.

There are 2 single 'O' words: **See Note 12**.

There are frequent changes from complex to simple, such as the melodramatic 'Come Viall' being followed by the simple 'what if this mixture ...': **See Note 21** (and it is these sudden changes that can give an age to the character, not the imposing of an image of 'young' onto her).

This speech is particularly embellished by editors, who add in a stage instruction to put down a dagger at the beginning, and change 'If I walke' to 'If I wake' — neither of these are necessary or add to the speech, where the first works just as well as a reference to the viall, and the second is an even more horrific image of sleep walking through the family mausoleum.

The Lamentable Tragedy
of Titus Andronicus, II-3

TAMORA

Have I not reason thinke you to looke pale.
These two have tic'd me hither to this place,
A barren, detested vale you see it is.
The Trees though Sommer, yet forlorne and leane,
Ore-come with Mosse, and baleful Misselto.
Heere never shines the Sunne, heere nothing breeds,
Unlesse the nightly Owle, or fatall Raven:
And when they shew'd me this abhorred pit,
They told me heere at dead time of the night,
A thousand Fiends, a thousand hissing Snakes,
Ten thousand swelling Toades, as many Urchins,
Would make such fearefull and confused cries,
As any mortall body hearing it,
Should straite fall mad, or else die suddenly.
No sooner had they told this hellish tale,
But strait they told me they would binde me heere,
Unto the body of a dismall yew,
And leave me to this miserable death.
And then they call'd me foule Adulteresse,
Lascivious Goth, and all the bitterest tearmes
That ever eare did heare to such effect.
And had you not by wondrous fortune come,
This vengeance on me had they executed:
Revenge it, as you love your Mothers life,
Or be ye not henceforth cal'd my Children.

FIRST FOLIO VERSE NOTES:

The speech starts off with 3 short thoughts, and then has one of 9 lines: **See Note 2**.

The capitals here are useful pointers to the attitude: **See Note 5**.

The whole speech is full of sharp consonants, including separations such as 'bitterest tearmes', that gives an overall effect to it: **See Note 20**.

The '-ed' endings need to be articulated: **See Note 7**, and there is a nice repetition of 'thousand': **See Note 13**.

'Urchins' = hedgehogs.

The Tragedie of Cymbeline, III-4

IMOGEN

Thou told'st me when we came from horse, the place
Was neere at hand: Ne're long'd my Mother so
To see me first, as I have now. *Pisanio*, Man:
Where is *Posthumus*? What is in thy mind
That makes thee stare thus? Wherefore breaks that sigh
From th'inward of thee? One, but painted thus
Would be interpreted a thing perplex'd
Beyond selfe-explication. Put thy selfe
Into a haviour of lesse feare, ere wildnesse
Vanquish my stayder Senses. What's the matter?
Why tender'st thou that Paper to me, with
A looke untender? If't be Summer Newes
Smile too't before: if Winterly, thou need'st
But keepe that count'nance stil. My Husbands hand?
That Drug-damn'd Italy, hath out-craftied him,
And hee's at some hard point. Speake man, thy Tongue
May take off some extreamitie, which to reade
Would be even mortall to me.

IMOGEN READES.

*Thy Mistris (Pisanio) hath plaide the Strumpet in my
Bed: the Testimonies whereof, lyes bleeding in me. I speak
not out of weake Surmises, but from proofe as strong as my
greefe, and as certaine as I expect my Revenge. That part, thou
(Pisanio) must acte for me, if thy Faith be not tainted with the
breach of hers; let thine owne hands take away her life: I shall
give thee opportunity at Milford Haven. She hath my Letter
for the purpose; where, if thou feare to strike, and to make mee
certaine it is done, thou art the Pander to her dishonour, and
equally to me disloyall.*

FIRST FOLIO VERSE NOTES:

The capitals are helpful to the meaning of the speech, and the letter she reads is printed in italics: **See Note 5**.

There are a lot of mid-line endings, all giving shape to the speech: **See Note 18**, and after a particularly breathless section comes a thought ending at the end of the line 'What's the matter?'.

The end words, often short ones, are at the end of a line for a good reason: **See Note 9**, and the long spelling for 'hee's at some hard point' both shows where the passion is, as well as introducing a series of assonances on the 'ee' sound: **See Notes 8 & 10**.

There are a number of abbreviated words 'told'st; tender'st; If't; too't; need'st' — again, giving a colour to the speech: **See Notes 8 & 23**.

The gap is where Pisanio speaks, and hands over the letter.

The Tragedie of Cymbeline, III-6

IMOGEN

I see a mans life is a tedious one,
I have tyr'd my selfe: and for two nights together
Have made the ground my bed.   I should be sicke,
But that my resolution helpes me: Milford,
When from the Mountaine top, *Pisanio* shew'd thee,
Thou was't within a kenne.   Oh Jove, I thinke
Foundations flye the wretched: such I meane,
Where they should be releev'd.   Two Beggers told me,
I could not misse my way.   Will poore Folkes lye
That have Afflictions on them, knowing 'tis
A punishment, or Triall?   Yes;   no wonder,
When Rich-ones scarse tell true.   To lapse in Fulnesse
Is sorer, then to lye for Neede: and Falshood
Is worse in Kings, then Beggers.   My deere Lord,
Thou art one o'th'false Ones: Now I thinke on thee,
My hunger's gone; but even before, I was
At point to sinke, for Food.   But what is this?
Heere is a path too't: 'tis some savage hold:
I were best not call; I dare not call: yet Famine
Ere cleane it o're-throw Nature, makes it valiant.
Plentie, and Peace breeds Cowards: Hardnesse ever
Of Hardinesse is Mother.   Hoa? who's heere?
If any thing that's civill, speake: if savage,
Take, or lend.   Hoa?   No answer?   Then Ile enter.
Best draw my Sword; and if mine Enemy
But feare the Sword like me, hee'l scarsely looke on't.
Such a Foe, good Heavens.

FIRST FOLIO VERSE NOTES:

This is a soliloquy: **See Note 25**.

Make sure that the first line is not acted with a full stop at the end of it: **See Note 2**.

There is a good pun at the beginning on 'tyr'd' meaning attired or dressed, and also meaning exhausted — and this will inform about her mood at the time: **See Note 15**.

There are a great number of mid-line endings: **See Note 18**, and there is no pause written in for when she shouts into the cave at the end — she just shouts and then carries on.

The last line being a half one could indicate a pause before speaking it: **See Note 17**.

The Tragedie of Cymbeline, IV-2

IMOGEN

IMOGEN AWAKES.

Yes Sir, to Milford-Haven, which is the way?
I thanke you: by yond bush? pray how farre thether?
'Ods pittikins: can it be sixe mile yet?
I have gone all night: 'Faith, Ile lye downe, and sleepe.
But soft; no Bedfellow?   Oh Gods, and Goddesses!
These Flowres are like the pleasures of the World;
This bloody man the care on't.   I hope I dreame:
For so I thought I was a Cave-keeper,
And Cooke to honest Creatures.   But 'tis not so:
'Twas but a bolt of nothing, shot at nothing,
Which the Braine makes of Fumes.   Our very eyes,
Are sometimes like our Judgements, blinde.   Good faith
I tremble still with feare: but if there be
Yet left in Heaven, as small a drop of pittie
As a Wrens eye; fear'd Gods, a part of it.
The Dreame's heere still: even when I wake it is
Without me, as within me: not imagin'd, felt.
A headlesse man?   The Garments of *Posthumus*?
I know the shape of's Legge: this is his Hand:
His Foote Mercuriall: his martiall Thigh
The brawnes of *Hercules*: but his Joviall face —
Murther in heaven?   How? 'tis gone. *Pisanio*,
All Curses madded *Hecuba* gave the Greekes,
And mine to boot, be darted on thee: thou
Conspir'd with that Irregulous divell *Cloten*,
Hath heere cut off my Lord.   To write, and read,
Be henceforth treacherous.   Damn'd *Pisanio*,
Hath with his forged Letters (damn'd *Pisanio*)

From this most bravest vessell of the world
Strooke the main top!   Oh *Posthumus*, alas,
Where is thy head? where's that?   Aye me! where's that?
Pisanio might have kill'd thee at the heart,
And left this head on.   How should this be, *Pisanio*?
'Tis he, and *Cloten*: Malice, and Lucre in them
Have laid this Woe heere.   Oh 'tis pregnant, pregnant!
The Drugge he gave me, which hee said was precious
And Cordiall to me, have I not found it
Murd'rous to'th'Senses?   That confirmes it home:
This is *Pisanio*'s deede, and *Cloten*: Oh!
Give colour to my pale cheeke with thy blood,
That we the horrider may seeme to those
Which chance to finde us.   Oh, my Lord! my Lord!

FIRST FOLIO VERSE NOTES:

This is a soliloquy: **See Note 25**, as Imogen awakes after being drugged.

The speech is stuffed with significant capitals and italics: **See Note 5**.

Although she wakes up next to the body of a headless man, the fluency and cleverness of the speech indicate a more complex attitude than mere horror: **See Note 21**.

The numerous mid-line endings add to the intensity of the speech: **See Note 18**, and the colons in unexpected places give the changing feelings: **See Notes 3 & 4**.

A famous actress admitted that she sometimes cut the 'Where is thy head?' line in case it got a laugh — but maybe this is what was originally intended.

''Ods pittikins' = God's pity; and 'pregnant' = obvious.

The Winters Tale, III-2

HERMIONE

Since what I am to say, must be but that
Which contradicts my Accusation, and
The testimonie on my part, no other
But what comes from my selfe, it shall scarce boot me
To say, Not guiltie: mine Integritie
Being counted Falsehood, shall (as I expresse it)
Be so receiv'd.   But thus, if Powres Divine
Behold our humane Actions (as they doe)
I doubt not then, but Innocence shall make
False Accusation blush, and Tyrannie
Tremble at Patience.   You (my Lord) best know
(Whom least will seeme to doe so) my past life
Hath beene as continent, as chaste, as true,
As I am now unhappy; which is more
Then Historie can patterne, though devis'd,
And play'd, to take Spectators.   For behold me,
A Fellow of the Royall Bed, which owe
A Moitie of the Throne: a great Kings Daughter,
The Mother to a hopefull Prince, here standing
To prate and talke for Life, and Honor, fore
Who please to come, and heare.   For Life, I prize it
As I weigh Griefe (which I would spare:) For Honor,
'Tis a derivative from me to mine,
And onely that I stand for.   I appeale
To your owne Conscience (Sir) before *Polixenes*
Came to your Court, how I was in your grace,
How merited to be so: Since he came,
With what encounter so uncurrant, I
Have strayn'd t'appeare thus; if one jot beyond
The bound of Honor, or in act, or will
That way enclining, hardned be the hearts
Of all that heare me, and my neer'st of Kin
Cry fie upon my Grave.

FIRST FOLIO VERSE NOTES:

The speech is full of long thoughts, not short statements, always ending in the middle of a line: **See Notes 2 & 18**.

The end words need to be chosen carefully, since they completely define the meaning, which is ruined if it is all run together, or enjambed: **See Note 9**.

The capitalised words and brackets add to the oration: **See Notes 5 & 16**.

The alliterations and assonances also clarify the intensity of the attitude, such as 'hardned/hearts/heare'; 'Kin/Cry/fie/my': **See Note 10**.

The repetition of the word 'as' gives a good build: **See Note 13**.

Editors change 'Whom least will seeme' to 'Who least will seeme'.

'boot' = profit; 'Moitie' = share.

The Winters Tale, III-2

HERMIONE

Sir, spare your Threats:
The Bugge which you would fright me with, I seeke:
To me can Life be no commoditie;
The crowne and comfort of my Life (your Favor)
I doe give lost, for I doe feele it gone,
But know not how it went.   My second Joy,
And first Fruits of my body, from his presence
I am bar'd, like one infectious.   My third comfort
(Star'd most unluckily) is from my breast
(The innocent milke in it most innocent mouth)
Hal'd out to murther.   My selfe on every Post
Proclaym'd a Strumpet: With immodest hatred
The Child-bed priviledge deny'd, which longs
To Women of all fashion.   Lastly, hurried
Here, to this place, i'th'open ayre, before
I have got strength of limit.   Now (my Liege)
Tell me what blessings I have here alive,
That I should feare to die?   Therefore proceed:
But yet heare this: mistake me not: no Life,
(I prize it not a straw) but for mine Honor,
Which I would free: if I shall be condemn'd
Upon surmizes (all proofes sleeping else,
But what your Jealousies awake) I tell you
'Tis Rigor, and not Law.   Your Honors all,
I doe referre me to the Oracle:
Apollo be my Judge.

FIRST FOLIO VERSE NOTES:

The pattern of this speech is for long thoughts to end in the middle of a line: **See Notes 2 & 18**.

There are several brackets: **See Note 16**.

The repetition of 'My', starting each time in the middle of a line, indicates both a build, as well as a determination that no-one shall be allowed to interrupt: **See Note 13**.

The 'Bugge' in the second line, if illustrated, shows that it is indeed a very small item: **See Note 24**.

The change in titles with which she addresses him 'Sir/my Liege' gives the progression to the attitude: **See Note 22**.

At the end, she suddenly changes from addressing him, to addressing the whole court — and it is, again, right in the middle of a line.

'longs' = belongs.

The Winters Tale, III-2

PAULINA

What studied torments (Tyrant) hast for me?
What Wheeles? Racks? Fires? What flaying? boyling?
In Leads, or Oyles?   What old, or newer Torture
Must I receive? whose every word deserves
To taste of thy most worst.   Thy Tyranny
(Together working with thy Jealousies,
Fancies too weake for Boyes, too greene and idle
For Girles of Nine) O thinke what they have done,
And then run mad indeed: starke-mad: for all
Thy by-gone fooleries were but spices of it.
That thou betrayed'st *Polixenes*, 'twas nothing,
(That did but shew thee, of a Foole, inconstant,
And damnable ingratefull:) Nor was't much.
Thou would'st have poyson'd good *Camillo's* Honor,
To have him kill a King: poore Trespasses,
More monstrous standing by: whereof I reckon
The casting forth to Crowes, thy Baby-daughter,
To be or none, or little; though a Devill
Would have shed water out of fire, ere don't:
Nor is't directly layd to thee, the death
Of the young Prince, whose honorable thoughts
(Thoughts high for one so tender) cleft the heart
That could conceive a grosse and foolish Sire
Blemish'd his gracious Dam: this is not, no,
Layd to thy answere: but the last: O Lords,
When I have said, cry woe: the Queene, the Queene,
The sweet'st, deer'st creature's dead: and vengeance for't
Not drop'd downe yet.

FIRST FOLIO VERSE NOTES:

The first few lines are full of capitals and, more importantly, question marks. Rigorously playing these gives an entirely fresh look to the speech: **See Note 5**.

There are then some very long thoughts: **See Note 2**, the first starting off in the middle of a line: **See Note 18**.

There is a good single 'O': **See Note 12**.

The end words are important for the meaning of the speech: **See Note 90**.

There are as well a large number of shortened words: 'was't; would'st; don't; is't; sweet'st; deer'st; for't': **See Notes 8 & 23**, make this speech very clipped and precise.

The Winters Tale, III-2

PAULINA

I say she's dead: Ile swear't. If word, nor oath
Prevaile not, go and see: if you can bring
Tincture, or lustre in her lip, her eye
Heate outwardly, or breath within, Ile serve you
As I would do the Gods. But, O thou Tyrant,
Do not repent these things, for they are heavier
Then all thy woes can stirre: therefore betake thee
To nothing but dispaire. A thousand knees,
Ten thousand yeares together, naked, fasting,
Upon a barren Mountaine, and still Winter
In storme perpetuall, could not move the Gods
To looke that way thou wer't.

I am sorry for't;
All faults I make, when I shall come to know them,
I do repent: Alas, I have shew'd too much
The rashnesse of a woman: he is toucht
To th'Noble heart. What's gone, and what's past helpe
Should be past greefe: Do not receive affliction
At my petition; I beseech you, rather
Let me be punish'd, that have minded you
Of what you should forget. Now (good my Liege)
Sir, Royall Sir, forgive a foolish woman:
The love I bore your Queene (Lo, foole againe)
Ile speake of her no more, nor of your Children:
Ile not remember you of my owne Lord,
(Who is lost too:) take your patience to you,
And Ile say nothing.

FIRST FOLIO VERSE NOTES:

The large number of mid-line endings immediately give a shape and colour to the speech: **See Note 18**.

The change in titles are fascinating 'Tyrant/my Liege/Sir/Royall Sir': **See Note 22**.

The end words are particularly important to the meaning and attitude: **See Note 9**.

The alliterations and assonances all clarify the feelings 'greefe/receive/beseech/me/Liege/Queene/ speake': **See Note 10**.

The separation 'lost too' is useful: **See Note 20**, and the 'then' is our modern 'than': **See Note 8**.

The gap is where there is an interruption by Leontes and the Lords, trying to stop her speaking.

The Winters Tale, IV-4

PERDITA

Ile not put
The Dible in earth, to set one slip of them:
No more then were I painted, I would wish
This youth should say 'twer well: and onely therefore
Desire to breed by me.   Here's flowres for you:
Hot Lavender, Mints, Savory, Marjorum,
The Mary-gold, that goes to bed with'Sun,
And with him rises, weeping: These are flowres
Of middle summer, and I thinke they are given
To men of middle age.   Y'are very welcome.

*(I should leave grasing, were I of your flocke,
And onely live by gazing.)*

Out alas:
You'ld be so leane, that blasts of January
Would blow you through and through.   Now (my fairst
                                    Friend,)
I would I had some Flowres o'th'Spring, that might
Become your time of day: and yours, and yours,
That weare upon your Virgin-branches yet
Your Maiden-heads growing: O *Proserpina*,
For the Flowres now, that (frighted) thou let'st fall
From *Dysses* Waggon: Daffadils,
That come before the Swallow dares, and take
The windes of March with beauty: Violets (dim,
But sweeter then the lids of *Juno's* eyes,
Or *Cytherea's* breath) pale Prime-roses,
That dye unmarried, ere they can behold
Bright Phœbus in his strength (a Maladie
Most incident to Maids:) bold Oxlips, and
The Crowne Imperiall: Lillies of all kinds,
(The Flowre-de-Luce being one.)   O, these I lacke,
To make you Garlands of, and my sweet friend,
To strew him o're, and ore.

FIRST FOLIO VERSE NOTES:

There is a lot of sexual innuendo (a dibble makes a hole in the ground): **See Note 15**.

The end words are specific to the sense: **See Note 9**. The whole speech is not just a list of flowers, but the imagery that goes with them: **See Note 14**.

The mid-line endings show that there is a drive to the speech, and the unexpected punctuation adds to the interpretation: **See Notes 4 & 18**.

There are 2 uses of the single 'O': **See Note 12**, and the interruption is spoken by Camillo.

The life and death of King John, III-1

CONSTANCE

Gone to be married?   Gone to sweare a peace?
False blood to false blood joyn'd.   Gone to be friends?
Shall *Lewis* have *Blaunch*, and *Blaunch* those Provinces?
It is not so, thou hast mispoke, misheard,
Be well advis'd, tell ore thy tale againe.
It cannot be, thou do'st but say 'tis so.
I trust I may not trust thee, for thy word
Is but the vaine breath of a common man:
Beleeve me, I doe not beleeve thee man,
I have a Kings oath to the contrarie.
Thou shalt be punish'd for thus frighting me,
For I am sicke, and capeable of feares,
Opprest with wrongs, and therefore full of feares,
A widdow, husbandles, subject to feares,
A woman naturally borne to feares;
And though thou now confesse thou didst but jest
With my vext spirits, I cannot take a Truce,
But they will quake and tremble all this day.
What dost thou meane by shaking of thy head?
Why dost thou looke so sadly on my sonne?
What meanes that hand upon that breast of thine?
Why holdes thine eie that lamentable rhewme,
Like a proud river peering ore his bounds?
Be these sad signes confirmers of thy words?
Then speake againe, not all thy former tale,
But this one word, whether thy tale be true.

FIRST FOLIO VERSE NOTES:

The first line has a mid-line ending, as does the second line: **See Note 18**.

There are repetitions of the word 'gone', and of other words all through the speech: **See Note 13**.

4 lines in a row end with the word 'feares': **See Notes 13 & 23**, and there is a sequence of 'What; Why; What; Why' starting 4 lines.

The questions should be acted as questions, and there are a *lot* of them: **See Note 23**.

There are many assonances and alliterations, and that in itself is a good clue: **See Note 10**.

The life and death of King John, III-1

CONSTANCE

A wicked day, and not a holy day.
What hath this day deserv'd? what hath it done,
That it in golden letters should be set
Among the high tides in the Kalender?
Nay, rather turne this day out of the weeke,
This day of shame, oppression, perjury.
Or if it must stand still, let wives with childe
Pray that their burthens may not fall this day,
Lest that their hopes prodigiously be crost:
But (on this day) let Sea-men feare no wracke,
No bargaines breake that are not this day made;
This day all things begun, come to ill end,
Yea, faith it selfe to hollow falshood change.

You have beguil'd me with a counterfeit
Resembling Majesty, which being touch'd and tride,
Proves valuelesse: you are forsworne, forsworne,
You came in Armes to spill mine enemies bloud,
But now in Armes, you strengthen it with yours.
The grapling vigor, and rough frowne of Warre
Is cold in amitie, and painted peace,
And our oppression hath made up this league:
Arme, arme, you heavens, against these perjur'd Kings,
A widdow cries, be husband to me (heavens)
Let not the howres of this ungodly day
Weare out the daies in Peace; but ere Sun-set,
Set armed discord 'twixt these perjur'd Kings,
Heare me, Oh, heare me.

FIRST FOLIO VERSE NOTES:

The repetition of the word 'day' 9 times sets the speech off: **See Note 13**.

The alliterations and assonances point up the speech: 'day/shame'; 'wives/childe'; 'bargaines/breake'; 'day/made'; 'faith/change' etc: **See Note 10**.

There are some nice separations, as in 'wicked day'; 'hath this'; 'letters should'; 'rough frowne': **See Note 20**.

The gap is where the King of France speaks of how he has helped her.

'daies' = days.

The life and death of King John, III-3

CONSTANCE

Thou art holy to belye me so,
I am not mad: this haire I teare is mine,
My name is *Constance,* I was *Geffreyes* wife,
Yong *Arthur* is my sonne, and he is lost:
I am not mad, I would to heaven I were,
For then 'tis like I should forget my selfe:
O, if I could, what griefe should I forget?
Preach some Philosophy to make me mad,
And thou shalt be Canoniz'd (Cardinall.)
For, being not mad, but sensible of greefe,
My reasonable part produces reason
How I may be deliver'd of these woes,
And teaches mee to kill or hang my selfe:
If I were mad, I should forget my sonne,
Or madly thinke a babe of clowts were he;
I am not mad: too well, too well I feele
The different plague of each calamitie.

(*Binde up your haires.*)

Yes that I will: and wherefore will I do it?
I tore them from their bonds, and cride aloud,
O, that these hands could so redeeme my sonne,
As they have given these hayres their libertie:
But now I envie at their libertie,
And will againe commit them to their bonds,
Because my poore childe is a prisoner.
And Father Cardinall, I have heard you say
That we shall see and know our friends in heaven:
If that be true, I shall see my boy againe;
For since the birth of *Caine*, the first male-childe
To him that did but yesterday suspire,
There was not such a gracious creature borne:

But now will Canker-sorrow eat my bud,
And chase the native beauty from his cheeke,
And he will looke as hollow as a Ghost,
As dim and meager as an Agues fitte,
And so hee'll dye: and rising so againe,
When I shall meet him in the Court of heaven
I shall not know him: therefore never, never
Must I behold my pretty *Arthur* more.

FIRST FOLIO VERSE NOTES:

The word 'mad' is repeated 7 times: **See Note 13**.

There is good alliteration: 'make me mad': **See Note 10**.

The long spelling of 'mee' is a good help: **See Note 6**, as is the single 'O': **See Note 12**.

The thoughts are all long ones — beware of putting in any full stops at the end of a line, and remember to choose the end words of a line: **See Notes 2 & 10**.

The line (with a few more) is spoken by the King of France.

'Ague' = sickness.

The life and death of King Richard the Second, I-2

DUTCHESSE OF GLOUCESTER

Findes brotherhood in thee no sharper spurre?
Hath love in thy old blood no living fire?
Edwards seven sonnes (whereof thy selfe art one)
Were as seven violles of his Sacred blood,
Or seven faire branches springing from one roote:
Some of those seven are dride by natures course,
Some of those branches by the destinies cut:
But *Thomas*, my deere Lord, my life, my Glouster,
One Violl full of *Edwards* Sacred blood,
One flourishing branch of his most Royall roote
Is crack'd, and all the precious liquor spilt;
Is hackt downe, and his summer leafes all vaded
By Envies hand, and Murders bloody Axe.
Ah *Gaunt*!   His blood was thine, that bed, that wombe,
That mettle, that selfe-mould that fashion'd thee,
Made him a man: and though thou liv'st, and breath'st,
Yet art thou slaine in him: thou dost consent
In some large measure to thy Fathers death,
In that thou seest thy wretched brother dye,
Who was the modell of thy Fathers life.
Call it not patience (*Gaunt*) it is dispaire,
In suffring thus thy brother to be slaughter'd,
Thou shew'st the naked pathway to thy life,
Teaching sterne murther how to butcher thee:
That which in meane men we intitle patience
Is pale cold cowardice in noble brests:
What shall I say, to safegard thine owne life,
The best way is to venge my Glousters death.

FIRST FOLIO VERSE NOTES:

There are a lot of repeated words in this speech: 'seven' and 'one' and 'that': **See Note 13**.

There is a nice separation at the beginning '*Edwards* seven' and later of '*Edwards* Sacred': **See Note 20**.

The build of titles she uses of '*Thomas*/Lord/life/Glouster' points to a political agenda: **See Notes 14 & 22**.

There are long thoughts in this speech, especially the one leading up to 'Murders bloody Axe': **See Note 2**.

The life and death of King Richard the Second, V-1

QUEENE

This way the King will come: this is the way
To *Julius Cæsars* ill-erected Tower:
To whose flint Bosome, my condemned Lord
Is doom'd a Prisoner, by prowd *Bullingbrooke*.
Here let us rest, if this rebellious Earth
Have any resting for her true Kings Queene.

ENTER RICHARD, AND GUARD.

But soft, but see, or rather doe not see,
My faire Rose wither: yet looke up; behold,
That you in pittie may dissolve to dew,
And wash him fresh againe with true-love Teares.
Ah thou, the Modell where old Troy did stand,
Thou Mappe of Honor, thou King *Richards* Tombe,
And not King *Richard*: thou most beauteous Inne,
Why should hard-favor'd Griefe be lodg'd in thee,
When Triumph is become an Ale-house Guest.

What, is my *Richard* both in shape and minde
Transform'd, and weaken'd?   Hath *Bullingbrooke*
Depos'd thine Intellect? hath he beene in thy Heart?
The Lyon dying, thrusteth forth his Paw,
And wounds the Earth, if nothing else, with rage
To be o're-powr'd: and wilt thou, Pupill-like,
Take thy Correction mildly, kisse the Rodde,
And fawne on Rage with base Humilitie,
Which art a Lyon, and a King of Beasts?

FIRST FOLIO VERSE NOTES:

The gap is where Richard speaks of his resignation to his fate.

After he enters, she has a long thought to speak: **See Note 2**.

There are a lot of images and metaphors chosen to describe the king, so the emotions cannot be simple ones: **See Note 21**.

Keep the '-ed' endings to make the verse regular: **See Note 7**.

The mid-line ending after 'weaken'd?' gives a wonderful impulse to the acting: **See Note 18**.

The First Part of Henry the Fourth, II-3

LADY PERCIE

O my good Lord, why are you thus alone?
For what offence have I this fortnight bin
A banish'd woman from my *Harries* bed?
Tell me (sweet Lord) what is't that takes from thee
Thy stomacke, pleasure, and thy golden sleepe?
Why dost thou bend thine eyes upon the earth?
And start so often when thou sitt'st alone?
Why hast thou lost the fresh blood in thy cheekes?
And given my Treasures and my rights of thee,
To thicke-ey'd musing, and curst melancholly?
In my faint-slumbers, I by thee have watcht,
And heard thee murmore tales of Iron Warres:
Speake tearmes of manage to thy bounding Steed,
Cry courage to the field.   And thou hast talk'd
Of Sallies, and Retires; Trenches, Tents,
Of Palizadoes, Frontiers, Parapets,
Of Basiliskes, of Canon, Culverin,
Of Prisoners ransome, and of Souldiers slaine,
And all the current of a headdy fight.
Thy spirit within thee hath beene so at Warre,
And thus hath so bestirr'd thee in thy sleepe,
That beds of sweate hath stood upon thy Brow,
Like bubbles in a late-disturbed Streame;
And in thy face strange motions have appear'd,
Such as we see when men restraine their breath
On some great sodaine hast.   O what portents are these?
Some heavie businesse hath my Lord in hand,
And I must know it: else he loves me not.

FIRST FOLIO VERSE NOTES:

The speech starts with a single 'O', and has a second one near the end: **See Note 12**.

She addresses him as 'you' in the first line, but then switches to 'thee' for the rest of the speech: **See Note 22**. She also calls him 'good Lord/my *Harries*/sweet Lord/my Lord': **See Note 14**.

There are a number of questions to be made questions, as well as 2 mid-line endings: **See Note 18**.

4 lines start with 'Of' — and the list they refer to is a precise and careful gradation of taking war from the fun part of 'Sallies, and Retires' through the practicalities of 'Frontiers, Parapets' into the realities of weapons to the results of war: 'Souldiers slaine.' **See Note 14**.

The Second Part of Henry the Fourth, II-3

LADY PERCIE

Oh yet, for heavens sake, go not to these Warrs;
The Time was (Father) when you broke your word,
When you were more endeer'd to it, then now,
When your owne Percy, when my heart-deere *Harry*,
Threw many a Northward looke, to see his Father
Bring up his Powres: but he did long in vaine.
Who then perswaded you to stay at home?
There were two Honors lost; Yours, and your Sonnes.
For Yours, may heavenly glory brighten it:
For His, it stucke upon him, as the Sunne
In the gray vault of Heaven: and by his Light
Did all the Chevalrie of England move
To do brave Acts.   He was (indeed) the Glasse
Wherein the Noble-Youth did dresse themselves.
He had no Legges, that practic'd not his Gate:
And speaking thicke (which Nature made his blemish)
Became the Accents of the Valiant.
For those that could speake low, and tardily,
Would turne their owne Perfection, to Abuse,
To seeme like him.   So that in Speech, in Gate,
In Diet, in Affections of delight,
In Militarie Rules, Humors of Blood,
He was the Marke, and Glasse, Coppy, and Booke,
That fashion'd others.   And him, O wondrous! him,
O Miracle of Men!   Him did you leave
(Second to none) un-seconded by you,
To looke upon the hideous God of Warre,
In dis-advantage, to abide a field,
Where nothing but the sound of *Hotspurs* Name
Did seeme defensible: so you left him.

Never, O never doe his Ghost the wrong,
To hold your Honor more precise and nice
With others, then with him.   Let them alone:
The Marshall and the Arch-bishop are strong.
Had my sweet *Harry* had but halfe their Numbers,
To day might I (hanging on *Hotspurs* Necke)
Have talk'd of *Monmouth's* Grave.

FIRST FOLIO VERSE NOTES:

The first version of this speech in the Quarto had 'for Gods sake' in the first line; the Folio would have changed that due to the Puritan's strictures on taking the name of the Lord in vain.

She refers to her dead husband in turn as 'Percy/*Harry*/*Hotspurs*/*Harry*/*Hotspurs*': **See Note 22**.

The single 'O''s brighten up the speech: **See Note 12**.

The capitals are instructive: **See Note 5**, and the end words are to be noted particularly: **See Note 9**.

There are a number of mid-line endings: **See Note 18**, and a number of brackets that pay dividends in being acknowledged: **See Note 16**.

The Life of Henry the Fift, Prologue

PROLOGUE

O For a Muse of Fire, that would ascend
The brightest Heaven of Invention:
A Kingdome for a Stage, Princes to Act,
And Monarchs to behold the swelling Scene.
Then should the Warlike *Harry*, like himselfe,
Assume the Port of *Mars*, and at his heeles
(Leasht in, like Hounds) should Famine, Sword, and Fire
Crouch for employment.   But pardon, Gentles all:
The flat unraysed Spirits, that hath dar'd,
On this unworthy Scaffold, to bring forth
So great an Object.   Can this Cock-Pit hold
The vastie fields of France?   Or may we cramme
Within this Woodden O, the very Caskes
That did affright the Ayre at Agincourt?
O pardon: since a crooked Figure may
Attest in little place a Million,
And let us, Cyphers to this great Accompt,
On your imaginarie Forces worke.
Suppose within the Girdle of these Walls
Are now confin'd two mightie Monarchies,
Whose high, up-reared, and abutting Fronts,
The perillous narrow Ocean parts asunder.
Peece out our imperfections with your thoughts:
Into a thousand parts divide one Man,
And make imaginarie Puissance.
Thinke when we talke of Horses, that you see them,
Printing their prowd Hoofes i'th'receiving Earth:
For 'tis your thoughts that now must deck our Kings,
Carry them here and there: Jumping o're Times;
Turning th'accomplishment of many yeeres
Into an Howre-glasse: for the which supplie,
Admit me *Chorus* to this Historie;

Who Prologue-like, your humble patience pray,
Gently to heare, kindly to judge our Play.

FIRST FOLIO VERSE NOTES:

This is a soliloquy: **See Note 25**, and it starts with a single 'O': **See Note 12** (although the 'Woodden O' refers to the Globe Theatre itself).

There are 3 important mid-line endings: **See Note 18**.

The sense of the speech is contained by *not* putting a full stop after the second line: **See Note 2**, and by carefully choosing the end words, especially on the first line: **See Note 9**.

The colons in the speech are of particular help: **See Note 3**.

The '-ed' endings need to be used: **See Note 7**.

There is a sudden gear change back to simple language after the flowery beginning: **See Note 21**.

'Port' = demeanor; 'Puissance' = troops.

The Life of Henry the Fift, I-6

HOSTESSE QUICKLY

Nay sure, hee's not in Hell: hee's in *Arthurs*
Bosome, if ever man went to *Arthurs* Bosome: a made a
finer end, and went away and it had beene any Christome
Child: a parted ev'n just betweene Twelve and One, ev'n
at the turning o'th'Tyde: for after I saw him fumble with
the Sheets, and play with Flowers, and smile upon his fingers end, I knew there was but one way: for his Nose was
as sharpe as a Pen, and a Table of greene fields.   How now
Sir *John* (quoth I?) what man? be a good cheare: so a
cryed out, God, God, God, three or foure times: now I,
to comfort him, bid him a should not thinke of God; I
hop'd there was no neede to trouble himselfe with any
such thoughts yet: so a bad me lay more Clothes on his
feet: I put my hand into the Bed, and felt them, and they
were as cold as any stone: then I felt to his knees, and so
up-peer'd, and upward, and all was as cold as any stone.

FIRST FOLIO VERSE NOTES:

This speech is all in prose: **<u>See Note 1</u>**, as she describes the death of Falstaffe.

At first, the reference is to 'hee', but later in the speech it is to the more colloquial 'a': **<u>See Note 8</u>**.

A Table is a book — and the imagery of 'a Table of greene fields' remains perfectly in harmony with the earlier 'Pen', even though editors without the slightest evidence change it to 'babbled of green fields'.

The repetition of 'stone' ties in with its Elizabethan meaning of 'testicles': **<u>See Notes 13 & 15</u>**.

The Life of Henry the Fift, II-Prologue

CHORUS

Thus with imagin'd wing our swift Scene flyes,
In motion of no lesse celeritie then that of Thought.
Suppose, that you have seene
The well-appointed King at Dover Peer,
Embarke his Royaltie: and his brave Fleet,
With silken Streamers, the young *Phebus* fayning;
Play with your Fancies: and in them behold,
Upon the Hempen Tackle, Ship-boyes climbing;
Heare the shrill Whistle, which doth order give
To sounds confus'd: behold the threaden Sayles,
Borne with th'invisible and creeping Wind,
Draw the huge Bottomes through the furrowed Sea,
Bresting the loftie Surge. O, doe but thinke
You stand upon the Rivage, and behold
A Citie on th'inconstant Billowes dauncing:
For so appeares this Fleet Majesticall,
Holding due course to Harflew. Follow, follow:
Grapple your minds to sternage of this Navie,
And leave your England as dead Mid-night, still,
Guarded with Grandsires, Babyes, and old Women,
Eyther past, or not arriv'd to pyth and puissance:
For who is he, whose Chin is but enricht
With one appearing Hayre, that will not follow
These cull'd and choyse-drawne Cavaliers to France?
Worke, worke your Thoughts, and therein see a Siege:
Behold the Ordenance on their Carriages,
With fatall mouthes gaping on girded Harflew.
Suppose th'Embassador from the French comes back:
Tells *Harry*, That the King doth offer him
Katherine his Daughter, and with her to Dowrie,

Some petty and unprofitable Dukedomes.
The offer likes not: and the nimble Gunner
With Lynstock now the divellish Cannon touches,

ALARUM, AND CHAMBERS GOE OFF.

And downe goes all before them.   Still be kind,
And eech out our performance with your mind.

FIRST FOLIO VERSE NOTES:

This is a soliloquy: **See Note 25**.

The 2nd line is very long, and the 3rd a half-line. Editors mistakenly 'regularise' these 2 lines, but the acting note from the Folio is to cram the second line, and to pause before the third: **See Note 17.**

The lengths of all the thoughts are precise, and important to acknowledge: **See Note 2**.

There is a good single 'O': **See Note 12**.

The mid-line endings tell where the pressure is to be maintained in the speech: **See Note 18**.

There is a nice rhyming couplet to end the speech: **See Note 11**.

Editors change 'Dover' to 'Hampton'; and 'fayning' to 'fanning'.

'Rivage' = shore.

The Life of Henry the Fift, III-Prologue

CHORUS

Now entertaine conjecture of a time,
When creeping Murmure and the poring Darke
Fills the wide Vessell of the Universe.
From Camp to Camp, through the foule Womb of Night
The Humme of eyther Army stilly sounds;
That the fixt Centinels almost receive
The secret Whispers of each others Watch.
Fire answers fire, and through their paly flames
Each Battaile sees the others umber'd face.
Steed threatens Steed, in high and boastfull Neighs
Piercing the Nights dull Eare: and from the Tents,
The Armourers accomplishing the Knights,
With busie Hammers closing Rivets up,
Give dreadfull note of preparation.
The Countrey Cocks doe crow, the Clocks doe towle:
And the third howre of drowsie Morning nam'd,
Prowd of their Numbers, and secure in Soule,
The confident and over-lustie French,
Doe the low-rated English play at Dice;
And chide the creeple-tardy-gated Night,
Who like a foule and ougly Witch doth limpe
So tediously away.   The poore condemned English,
Like Sacrifices, by their watchfull Fires
Sit patiently, and inly ruminate
The Mornings danger: and their gesture sad,
Investing lanke-leane Cheekes, and Warre-worne Coats,
Presented them unto the gazing Moone
So many horride Ghosts.   O now, who will behold
The Royall Captaine of this ruin'd Band
Walking from Watch to Watch, from Tent to Tent;
Let him cry, Prayse and Glory on his head:
For forth he goes, and visits all his Hoast,
Bids them good morrow with a modest Smyle,

And calls them Brothers, Friends, and Countreymen.
Upon his Royall Face there is no note,
How dread an Army hath enrounded him;
Nor doth he dedicate one jot of Colour
Unto the wearie and all-watched Night:
But freshly lookes, and over-beares Attaint,
With chearefull semblance, and sweet Majestie:
That every Wretch, pining and pale before,
Beholding him, plucks comfort from his Lookes.
A Largesse universall, like the Sunne,
His liberall Eye doth give to every one,
Thawing cold feare, that meane and gentle all
Behold, as may unworthinesse define.
A little touch of *Harry* in the Night,
And so our Scene must to the Battaile flye:
Where, O for pitty, we shall much disgrace,
With foure or five most vile and ragged foyles,
(Right ill dispos'd, in brawle ridiculous)
The Name of Agincourt: Yet sit and see,
Minding true things, by what their Mock'ries bee.

FIRST FOLIO VERSE NOTES:

As with all soliloquies: **See Note 25**, the arguments and structure of the speech are carefully defined by the lengths of thought: **See Note 2**.

It is also illuminated by which words end each line: **See Note 9**.

The assonances and alliterations 'Whispers/Watch'; 'paly/flames' give intimacy to the speech: **See Note 10**.

There are 2 single 'O''s to play with: **See Note 12**.

The traditional editors put 'A little touch of *Harry* in the Night,' at the end of the previous thought; here in the Folio it is the start of a new thought, and it plays beautifully: **See Note 4**.

The first Part of Henry the Sixt, I-2

JOANE PUZEL

Dolphin, I am by birth a Shepheards Daughter,
My wit untrayn'd in any kind of Art:
Heaven and our Lady gracious hath it pleas'd
To shine on my contemptible estate.
Loe, whilest I wayted on my tender Lambes,
And to Sunnes parching heat display'd my cheekes,
Gods Mother deigned to appeare to me,
And in a Vision full of Majestie,
Will'd me to leave my base Vocation,
And free my Countrey from Calamitie:
Her ayde she promis'd, and assur'd successe.
In compleat Glory shee reveal'd her selfe:
And whereas I was black and swart before,
With those cleare Rayes, which shee infus'd on me,
That beautie am I blest with, which you may see.
Aske me what question thou canst possible,
And I will answer unpremeditated:
My Courage trie by Combat, if thou dar'st,
And thou shalt finde that I exceed my Sex.
Resolve on this, thou shalt be fortunate,
If thou receive me for thy Warlike Mate.

FIRST FOLIO VERSE NOTES:

This is spoken in verse, which in itself gives a clue as to the abilities of Joane: **See Note 1**.

The words in capitals help the understanding: **See Note 5**.

The thoughts are longer than might be imagined, especially the one that ends 'assur'd successe': **See Note 2**.

The alliterations work well for the character 'Loe/ Lambes; whilest/wayted': **See Note 10**.

She addresses the Dolphin first as 'you' but ends up with a whole series of 'thee's': **See Note 22**.

Dolphin was the traditional English name for the son of the French King, or Dauphin.

The second Part of Henry the Sixt, I-3

QUEENE MARGARET

My Lord of Suffolke, say, is this the guise?
Is this the Fashions in the Court of England?
Is this the Government of Britaines Ile?
And this the Royaltie of *Albions* King?
What, shall King *Henry* be a Pupill still,
Under the surly *Glosters* Governance?
Am I a Queene in Title and in Stile,
And must be made a Subject to a Duke?
I tell thee *Poole,* when in the Citie *Tours*
Thou ran'st a-tilt in honor of my Love,
And stol'st away the Ladies hearts of France;
I thought King *Henry* had resembled thee,
In Courage, Courtship, and Proportion:
But all his minde is bent to Holinesse,
To number *Ave-Maries* on his Beades:
His Champions, are the Prophets and Apostles,
His Weapons, holy Sawes of sacred Writ,
His Studie is his Tilt-yard, and his Loves
Are brazen Images of Canonized Saints.
I would the Colledge of the Cardinalls
Would chuse him Pope, and carry him to Rome,
And set the Triple Crowne upon his Head;
That were a State fit for his Holinesse.

FIRST FOLIO VERSE NOTES:

The word 'this' is repeated in each of the first 4 lines: **See Note 13**, and the first time it is used there is a nice assonance 'is this': **See Note 10**.

She starts by calling him 'Lord of Suffolke', but then switches to his family name '*Poole*': **See Note 22**.

The capitals are useful for the sense, and the italics are proper names or foreign words: **See Note 5**.

There is a delightful series of antitheses (opposites) as Margaret compares what Henry should be doing, and what he does — but even here it is important to note that they are not in a consistent order; sometimes it is the war image first, sometimes the religious one: **See Note 4**.

The third Part of Henry the Sixt, I-4

QUEENE MARGARET

Brave Warriors, *Clifford* and *Northumberland*,
Come make him stand upon this Mole-hill here,
That raught at Mountaines with out-stretched Armes,
Yet parted but the shadow with his Hand.
What, was it you that would be Englands King?
Was't you that revell'd in our Parliament,
And made a Preachment of your high Descent?
Where are your Messe of Sonnes, to back you now?
The wanton *Edward*, and the lustie *George*?
And where's that valiant Crook-back Prodigie,
Dickie, your Boy, that with his grumbling voyce
Was wont to cheare his Dad in Mutinies?
Or with the rest, where is your Darling, *Rutland* ?
Looke *Yorke*, I stayn'd this Napkin with the blood
That valiant *Clifford*, with his Rapiers point,
Made issue from the Bosome of the Boy:
And if thine eyes can water for his death,
I give thee this to drie thy Cheekes withall.
Alas poore *Yorke*, but that I hate thee deadly,
I should lament thy miserable state.
I prythee grieve, to make me merry, *Yorke*.
What, hath thy fierie heart so parcht thine entrayles,
That not a Teare can fall, for *Rutlands* death?
Why art thou patient, man? thou should'st be mad:
And I, to make thee mad, doe mock thee thus.
Stampe, rave, and fret, that I may sing and dance.
Thou would'st be fee'd, I see, to make me sport:
Yorke cannot speake, unlesse he weare a Crowne.
A Crowne for *Yorke* ; and Lords, bow lowe to him:
Hold you his hands, whilest I doe set it on.

I marry Sir, now lookes he like a King:
I, this is he that tooke King *Henries* Chaire,
And this is he was his adopted Heire.
But how is it, that great *Plantagenet*
Is crown'd so soone, and broke his solemne Oath?
As I bethinke me, you should not be King,
Till our King *Henry* had shooke hands with Death.
And will you pale your head in *Henries* Glory,
And rob his Temples of the Diademe,
Now in his Life, against your holy Oath?
Oh 'tis a fault too too unpardonable.
Off with the Crowne; and with the Crowne, his Head,
And whilest we breathe, take time to doe him dead.

FIRST FOLIO VERSE NOTES:

She starts off by addressing her fellows as 'Warriors' —
a note as to what she expects of them: **See Note 22**, and
each son of Yorke is referred to by name, except Richard
who is called by his nick-name.

A mole hill is very small, and by acting it the image is all the
more insulting: **See Note 24**.

There are a lot of 'm' words to begin with: **See Note 10**,
and the words in capitals, such as 'Messe of Sonnes' add
to the understanding: **See Note 5**.

At first she addresses him as 'you', but then switches to
'thee', but brings it back to 'you' for the end when she puts
the paper crown on his head: **See Note 22**.

A nursery rhyme type of couplet in the middle 'Chaire/
Heire' gives an indication of her attitude: **See Note 11**, as
does the couplet that ends the speech.

'raught' = reached.

The Tragedy of Richard the Third, I-2

LADY ANNE

Set downe, set downe your honourable load,
If Honor may be shrowded in a Herse;
Whil'st I a-while obsequiously lament
Th'untimely fall of Vertuous Lancaster.
Poore key-cold Figure of a holy King,
Pale Ashes of the House of Lancaster;
Thou bloodlesse Remnant of that Royall Blood,
Be it lawfull that I invocate thy Ghost,
To heare the Lamentations of poore *Anne*,
Wife to thy *Edward*, to thy slaughtred Sonne,
Stab'd by the selfesame hand that made these wounds.
Loe, in these windowes that let forth thy life,
I powre the helplesse Balme of my poore eyes.
O cursed be the hand that made these holes:
Cursed the Heart, that had the heart to do it:
Cursed the Blood, that let this blood from hence:
More direfull hap betide that hated Wretch
That makes us wretched by the death of thee,
Then I can wish to Wolves, to Spiders, Toades,
Or any creeping venom'd thing that lives.
If ever he have Childe, Abortive be it,
Prodigeous, and untimely brought to light,
Whose ugly and unnaturall Aspect
May fright the hopefull Mother at the view,
And that be Heyre to his unhappinesse.
If ever he have Wife, let her be made
More miserable by the death of him,
Then I am made by my young Lord, and thee.
Come now towards Chertsey with your holy Lode,
Taken from Paules, to be interred there.

And still as you are weary of this waight,
Rest you, whiles I lament King *Henries* Coarse.

FIRST FOLIO VERSE NOTES:

The speech starts with a repeated word, and the actor must act a reason why it is repeated: **See Note 13**.

The speech is full of alliterations, assonances, and clever uses of words, all of which must be part of the attitude behind it; the mistake is to play from the sense, and try to play 32 lines sadly: **See Notes 10 & 21**. In particular, there is a run of 's' words, and then of 'h' words, finally a run of 'm' words.

There is a wonderful play on words 'I powre; poore eyes' that again point to this being a more conscious piece than simple emotion: **See Note 15**.

The repetition of all these clues seem to push this speech more to a public outcry rather than a private grief: **See Note 23**.

'Loe, in these windowes' indicates that she is directly pointing out to the audience the stab wounds in the body, which might need to be lifted up if all are to see what she is demonstrating: **See Note 24**.

Editors change 'More miserable by the death of him' to 'More miserable by the life of him'.

'hap betide' = fortune befall.

The Tragedy of Richard the Third, I-2

LADY ANNE

What do you tremble? are you all affraid?
Alas, I blame you not, for you are Mortall,
And Mortall eyes cannot endure the Divell.
Avant thou dreadfull minister of Hell;
Thou had'st but power over his Mortall body,
His Soule thou canst not have: Therefore be gone.

(*Sweet Saint, for Charity, be not so curst.*)

Foule Divell,
For Gods sake hence, and trouble us not,
For thou hast made the happy earth thy Hell:
Fill'd it with cursing cries, and deepe exclaimes:
If thou delight to view thy heynous deeds,
Behold this patterne of thy Butcheries.
Oh Gentlemen, see, see dead *Henries* wounds,
Open their congeal'd mouthes, and bleed afresh.
Blush, blush, thou lumpe of fowle Deformitie:
For 'tis thy presence that exhales this blood
From cold and empty Veines where no blood dwels.
Thy Deeds inhumane and unnaturall,
Provokes this Deluge most unnaturall.
O God! which this Blood mad'st, revenge his death:
O Earth! which this Blood drink'st, revenge his death.
Either Heav'n with Lightning strike the murth'rer dead:
Or Earth gape open wide, and eate him quicke,
As thou dost swallow up this good Kings blood,
Which his Hell-govern'd arme hath butchered.

FIRST FOLIO VERSE NOTES:

In the first part she addresses her followers as 'you', and Richard with the more intimate 'thee' – and this continues into the second part: **See Note 22**.

There is a wonderful repetition of 'Mortall': **See Note 13**.

There is also repetition of the word 'unnaturall', followed by the repetition of the single 'O', all of which give insight into the nature of the emotion and attitude: **See also Notes 12 & 23**. There is yet another repetition - 'revenge his death'.

In the second part of the speech, it is all one thought leading up to 'Butcheries': **See Note 2**.

The '-ed' will need to be used for 'butchered' at the end of the piece: **See Note 7**.

The line is spoken by Richard.

The Tragedy of Richard the Third, I-3

QUEENE MARGARET

What? were you snarling all before I came,
Ready to catch each other by the throat,
And turne you all your hatred now on me?
Did *Yorkes* dread Curse prevaile so much with Heaven,
That *Henries* death, my lovely *Edwards* death,
Their Kingdomes losse, my wofull Banishment,
Should all but answer for that peevish Brat?
Can Curses pierce the Clouds, and enter Heaven?
Why then give way dull Clouds to my quick Curses.
Though not by Warre, by Surfet dye your King,
As ours by Murther, to make him a King.
Edward thy Sonne, that now is Prince of Wales,
For *Edward* our Sonne, that was Prince of Wales,
Dye in his youth, by like untimely violence.
Thy selfe a Queene, for me that was a Queene,
Out-live thy glory, like my wretched selfe:
Long may'st thou live, to wayle thy Childrens death,
And see another, as I see thee now,
Deck'd in thy Rights, as thou art stall'd in mine.
Long dye thy happie dayes, before thy death,
And after many length'ned howres of griefe,
Dye neyther Mother, Wife, nor Englands Queene.
Rivers and *Dorset*, you were standers by,
And so wast thou, Lord *Hastings*, when my Sonne
Was stab'd with bloody Daggers: God, I pray him,
That none of you may live his naturall age,
But by some unlook'd accident cut off.

FIRST FOLIO VERSE NOTES:

The thoughts go on for longer than might be expected: **See Note 2**.

The clear alliterations through the piece such as 'Banishment/Brat'; 'Curses/Clouds'; the same with the assonances such as 'by like untimely violence' give the whole a great colour: **See Note 10**.

Noting the capitals, especially with 'Surfet', clarify the ideas and argument: **See Note 5**.

The speech starts with 'you' when she is addressing the group, but switches to 'thy' when she talks to Queene Elizabeth, then to 'you' for Rivers and Dorset, back to 'thy' for Hastings, and finally back again to 'you' for the general curse: **See Note 22**.

The Tragedy of Richard the Third, IV-3

QUEENE MARGARET

I call'd thee then, vaine flourish of my fortune:
I call'd thee then, poore Shadow, painted Queen,
The presentation of but what I was;
The flattering Index of a direfull Pageant;
One heav'd a high, to be hurl'd downe below:
A Mother onely mockt with two faire Babes;
A dreame of what thou wast, a garish Flagge
To be the ayme of every dangerous Shot;
A signe of Dignity, a Breath, a Bubble;
A Queene in jeast, onely to fill the Scene.
Where is thy Husband now?   Where be thy Brothers?
Where be thy two Sonnes?   Wherein dost thou Joy?
Who sues, and kneeles, and sayes, God save the Queene?
Where be the bending Peeres that flattered thee?
Where be the thronging Troopes that followed thee?
Decline all this, and see what now thou art.
For happy Wife, a most distressed Widdow:
For joyfull Mother, one that wailes the name:
For one being sued too, one that humbly sues:
For Queene, a very Caytiffe, crown'd with care:
For she that scorn'd at me, now scorn'd of me:
For she being feared of all, now fearing one:
For she commanding all, obey'd of none.
Thus hath the course of Justice whirl'd about,
And left thee but a very prey to time,
Having no more but Thought of what thou wast.
To torture thee the more, being what thou art,
Thou didst usurpe my place, and dost thou not
Usurpe the just proportion of my Sorrow?
Now thy proud Necke, beares halfe my burthen'd yoke,
From which, even heere I slip my wearied head,
And leave the burthen of it all, on thee.

Farwell Yorkes wife, and Queene of sad mischance,
These English woes, shall make me smile in France.

FIRST FOLIO VERSE NOTES:

The first 2 lines begin with 'I call'd thee then', and this is deliberate, not accidental: **See Note 13**.

The first 10 lines are all one thought: **See Note 2**, and this is followed by 7 questions, and then comes a list of 7 comparisons: **See Note 23**, each starting with 'For'.

The questions need to be made questions, and they are given added urgency by observing the mid-line endings: **See Note 18**.

All through the speech the capitals clarify the argument, and importance of each image: **See Note 5**.

The whole speech ends with a rhyming couplet: **See Note 11**.

'Caytiffe' = pitiful wretch.

The Famous History of the Life of King Henry the Eight, II-4

QUEENE KATHERINE

*THE QUEENE RISES OUT OF HER CHAIRE, AND
KNEELES AT THE KING'S FEETE.*

Sir, I desire you do me Right and Justice,
And to bestow your pitty on me; for
I am a most poore Woman, and a Stranger,
Borne out of your Dominions: having heere
No Judge indifferent, nor no more assurance
Of equall Friendship and Proceeding. Alas Sir:
In what have I offended you?   What cause
Hath my behaviour given to your displeasure,
That thus you should proceede to put me off,
And take your good Grace from me?   Heaven witnesse,
I have bene to you, a true and humble Wife,
At all times to your will conformable:
Ever in feare to kindle your Dislike,
Yea, subject to your Countenance: Glad, or sorry,
As I saw it inclin'd?   When was the houre
I ever contradicted your Desire?
Or made it not mine too?   Or which of your Friends
Have I not strove to love, although I knew
He were mine Enemy?   What Friend of mine,
That had to him deriv'd your Anger, did I
Continue in my Liking?   Nay, gave notice
He was from thence discharg'd? Sir, call to minde,
That I have beene your Wife, in this Obedience,
Upward of twenty yeares, and have bene blest
With many Children by you. If in the course
And processe of this time, you can report,

And prove it too, against mine Honor, aught;
My bond to Wedlocke, or my Love and Dutie
Against your Sacred Person; in Gods name
Turne me away: and let the foul'st Contempt
Shut doore upon me, and so give me up
To the sharp'st kinde of Justice.   Please you, Sir,
The King your Father, was reputed for
A Prince most Prudent; of an excellent
And unmatch'd Wit, and Judgement.   *Ferdinand*
My Father, King of Spaine, was reckon'd one
The wisest Prince, that there had reign'd, by many
A yeare before.   It is not to be question'd,
That they had gather'd a wise Councell to them
Of every Realme, that did debate this Businesse,
Who deem'd our Marriage lawful.   Wherefore I humbly
Beseech you Sir, to spare me, till I may
Be by my Friends in Spaine, advis'd; whose Counsaile
I will implore.   If not, i'th'name of God
Your pleasure be fulfill'd.

FIRST FOLIO VERSE NOTES:

The end words in each line are particularly important: **See Note 9**.

All the thoughts end in the middle of a line, which gives a great drive to the whole speech: **See Note 18**.

The capitalized words are a good guide to the ideas in the speech: **See Note 5**.

She addresses him throughout as 'Sir', almost too often, with a nice separation with 'Alas Sir': **See Note 20**.

The questions must be acted as questions, giving an ironic edge to the speech.

The Shakespearean Verse Acting Check List

An approach to acting Shakespearean text; work through the following points in order:

A. Identify whether the piece is in prose or poetry — and make the appropriate acting conclusions — especially if you go from one to the other in a scene or part.

B. Remember: the passion is in the PUNCTUATION! The whole thought continues until the first *full stop* (or, in North American, the first *period*): [**.**]. Sometimes (if the next word begins with a Capital) the end of a thought is a *question mark*: [**?**], or an *exclamation mark*: [**!**]. If the thought is complicated, it may be made up of several sentences, joined together with *colons*: [**:**], or *semi-colons*: [**;**]. These are *less* than a full stop, and are *not* the end of the thought. A *colon* is similar to the words: 'therefore', or: 'because'; while a *semi-colon* is similar to: 'and'. A *colon* can sometimes be where a thought is broken, where the speaker's thoughts go off in another direction.

C. *Before* looking at the speech for the very first time, *highlight* the three words leading up to the end of a thought, so that you have the correct lengths of thought the very first time you read the speech. Often these words are what that particular thought is all about — so go through the speech just reading them out, to get a pattern for the whole speech. Notice where a thought ends in the middle of a line (a mid-line ending) and make sure you *do* something about this — *why* does your character want/need to come in with the next thought so quickly?

D. Go through the speech, reading aloud all the words that are in Capitals that are not at the start of a line — this will give you a series of stepping stones that again will help to show a pattern for the whole speech.

E. Notice what title you give to the person you are speaking to, whether it is 'thee' or 'you' (and if it changes in the speech); whether you address them in a consistent way, or whether it changes within the speech — and so shows a changing attitude.

F. Saying it out loud, find the masculine and feminine endings (and the Alexandrines!) and so choose the final word in each verse line or not, as appropriate.

G. By saying it out loud, find the verbal conceits: that is, the rhymes, alliterations, assonances, and repeated words. These help you to decide which words to choose. Remember, to choose is not simply to emphasise — choice *can* be by emphasis, but it can also be done with de-emphasis, changes in pitch or tone, or by pausing. These individual choices are up to the performer to decide — and the best way to do *that* is to rely on instinct — to do what you *feel*. This also applies to words you don't understand — what does their sound make you *feel*?

H. Saying it out loud, choose the similes, metaphors, the strange words, and words with double meanings – especially the bawdy ones.

I. Saying it out loud, find the rhythm breaks and changes, the full or half lines, and see what they are telling you, where you pause for business (never just a pause). Remember, a half-line at the start or finish of a speech is generally not a pause, but a note to join on with other speeches.

J. By doing all the above, and making all those choices, find the changing attitudes. Particularly notice when the language changes from simple to complex, and vice versa, as indications where the character is being straight forward, or not. (Saying complicated and witty lines 'sincerely' merely means doing them *untruthfully* and *badly.*)

K. *All* clues are there not just to be identified, but to inspire an acting choice — the audience cannot see inside your mind, so if they do not get it — forget it! More is more — three words alliterating is a bigger clue than two; repeating the same word seven times in a speech is a bigger clue than five times. Bigger clues need larger theatricalisations!

L. By doing all the above with the changing attitudes, find the character by making all these words and choices your own. *In other words, find the acting reason for your character to say these lines in this way and at this time.*

M. Finally, speed it all up – amazingly. THIS is what makes it take off and fly — *without* having to tone down the verse work to make it 'real' or 'sincere' — and then the words will start acting YOU.

First Line Index

The line in brackets indicates either a famous line in the body of the speech, or that the speech actually starts with this other line.

Remember that in Elizabethan printing, the letter 'I' can stand either for first person singular (I), or for Aye (yes). I have not chosen which: that is your — the performer's — job to decide which is the appropriate choice. After 1603, there came an injunction not to use the Lord's name in vain, so that in the First Folio occasionally the word 'Heaven' is substituted for 'God'. Again, I have left this as in the Folio.